SHAKESPEARE TALES

TRAGEDIES

Andrew Lynn has a Ph.D. in Renaissance literature from Cambridge University. He now works to help resolve international and cross-border disputes.

www.andrewlynn.com

Shakespeare Tales

Tragedies

Charles and Mary Lamb

Edited with introductions by Andrew Lynn

HOWGILL
HOUSE

Howgill House Books

www.howgillhousebooks.com

Copyright © Andrew Lynn 2018

ISBN 978-1-912360-11-6

CONTENTS

INTRODUCTION

GENERAL INTRODUCTION

We all want to know Shakespeare.

Of all the great writers, there is none whose influence has spread as far and wide as that of Shakespeare. So profound has been his impact on the culture of the English speaking world, and beyond, that a life lived without some exposure to his work is hard to imagine. To have a passing familiarity with Romeo's passion, Hamlet's introspection, Othello's jealousy, and Lear's rage, is part of the common birthright of humanity. Every one of us is in a position to marvel at Cleopatra's barge burning on the waters of the Nile 'like a burnished throne', to recoil in disgust at Shylock's bloodlust for his 'pound of flesh', to exclaim at Petruchio's 'taming' of his wife through shockingly unmodern methods, to laugh aloud at the love affair between a fairy queen and a bumpkin with a donkey's head one midsummer night near Athens, and to smile darkly at the antics of Richard III seducing a woman whose husband, father,

1

and father-in-law he has all killed at the very funeral procession of the last of those his victims.

That Shakespeare stands at the forefront of world literature has never been seriously disputed. But what is it that almost four centuries after his death continues to draw us back to these works?

For some of us, it is the immensity of Shakespeare's vision and the unparalleled diversity of the worlds he creates and the characters with which he inhabits them. Shakespeare's dramatic journey begins with playful early comedies and thought-provoking histories, passes into a fully-fledged middle period giving rise to profound and disturbing tragedies as well as comedies and histories of a more sophisticated quality, and concludes with his several late romances full of nuance and mystery. We are transported in the comedies to Verona, Padua, Milan, and Messina in Italy, to Ephesus in Greece, to Navarre in northern Spain, and to the quasi-mystical Illyria on the Balkan Peninsula, as well as to the more homely town of Windsor back in England; in the tragedies we journey to the Kingdom of Denmark, the Republic of Venice, the remote Scottish highlands around Inverness, and the castles, heaths, and battlegrounds of ancient Britain; in the classical plays and histories we travel back in time to Rome, Athens, Egypt, and Troy of antiquity, as well as to England of the late Middle Ages; and in the romances we set sail for exotic lands edging the Mediterranean, remote and magical desert

2

islands, and forgotten kingdoms shrouded in the mists of prehistory.

For some of us, on the other hand, what draws us in is the sheer profundity of Shakespeare's work. At every turn, we are confronted with the deep questions of human existence: What is the essence of the human condition? Is there a natural order? What is a man? What is a woman? Our ethics and moral norms are interrogated: What is honour? When must we be loyal and when is it right to rebel? Is it ever right to enact revenge? What are the rewards, if any, of virtue? Political philosophies are cast against each other: monarchism and the divine right of kings meet republicanism and a nascent bourgeois order. Above all, Shakespeare's characters come alive as if born fully formed: overvaunting Macbeth, ludicrous Bottom, introspective Hamlet, melancholic Jacques, treacherous Iago, languorous Cleopatra, and malicious hunchbacked Richard III, among many others, come into being before us with as much vigour as at any time since the turn of the seventeenth century. Shakespeare's contemporary, Ben Jonson, famously said of the Bard: 'He was not of an age, but for all time'. The last 400 years, at least, have tended to bear that contention out.

And for some of us, what makes Shakespeare so compelling is the sheer range and originality of his language. In the first place, there is Shakespeare's legendary vocabulary. Recent studies have taken a more conservative view than those of the past, but even so, Shakespeare's vocabulary of 17,000 to 20,000 words compares favourably to the King James Bible, for example, which makes do with a mere 6,000. But Shakespeare did not just make use of the English language; he also helped to bring it into being. He was a relentless coiner of new words: the Oxford English Dictionary lists 2035 instances where Shakespeare is the first recorded user of a word, compared to about 500 instances for his contemporary, Spencer, 400 for Sidney, and about 50 for the King James Bible. When we say that the 'game is up' (*Cymbeline*) or that 'brevity is the soul of wit' (*Hamlet*); when we see a man 'play fast and loose' (*King John*) or 'hoist with his own petard' (*Hamlet*); when we feel for our 'own flesh and blood' (*The Merchant of Venice*) or are stricken by the 'green-eyed monster' of jealousy (*Othello*); and when we desire 'too much of a good thing' (*As You Like It*) or 'make a virtue of necessity' (*The Two Gentlemen of Verona*)—we are vehicles for Shakespeare's tongue and living testaments to his longevity. Shakespeare breathed life into the language like none other before or since.

To have read and comprehensively understood the thirty-seven plays that Shakespeare is generally accepted to have written would be the work of a lifetime for an industrious scholar. But to know some of the highlights and the broad features of his work is within the reach of all.

The book you now hold in your hands does that by providing classic and elegant prose renditions of

Shakespeare's plays. It is one of a series of five, each focused on a particular genre, which collectively covers the entire Shakespearean dramatic oeuvre: Comedies, Tragedies, Tragicomedies, Roman Tales, and English Histories. By gathering the tales together by genre, we can better appreciate how Shakespeare leads us through several stages of maturation to progressively deepen our experience with the reality he seeks to convey: comedy gives way to the difficulties of tragedy, the ambiguities of tragicomedy, the complexities of history and the bitter-sweet tonalities of romance, much as childhood gives way to adulthood and old age. It is characteristically Shakespearean that his mature vision as expressed in the late plays was neither comic nor tragic but romantic and tragicomic. If there is a final Shakespearean assessment of the human condition, it is that life sends ample measure of both sunshine and showers.

For the most part, the tales provided are the classic nineteenth-century prose versions penned by Charles and Mary Lamb. These versions were intended, in that day and age, to introduce Shakespeare's work to children. This fact should in no way deter the twenty-first-century adult from using them as his or her gateway to the Bard: these versions are adult in style and tone and are totally remote from what we think of today as 'children's literature'. What renders the Lamb versions timeless is their double grace: on the one hand they provide an effortless and pleasurable entry point to the great works of this complex and profound creator, while at the same time preserving, as far as possible, the expressive texture of Shakespeare's own words. The Lambs explain that their versions should not be the end point of the reader's journey: first read the prose tales, they suggest, to obtain a notion of the stories in general; next, explore passages and extracts from the original plays, which stand to be better enjoyed and understood in the light of that general understanding; finally, they suggest, it will be time to turn to the works in full to really experience the 'infinite variety' of Shakespeare's world.

The problem with the Lamb tales is that they are incomplete. Their *Tales from Shakespeare* contains twenty tales of the thirty-seven that we can confidently say Shakespeare wrote. It contains most (but not all) of the comedies: *As You Like It*, *The Comedy of Errors*, *A Midsummer Night's Dream*, *Much Ado About Nothing*, *The Taming of the Shrew*, *Twelfth Night*, and *The Two Gentlemen of Verona* are there; *Love's Labour's Lost* and *The Merry Wives of Windsor* are missing. The tragedies are well represented: *Hamlet*, *King Lear*, *Macbeth*, *Othello*, *Romeo and Juliet*, and *Timon of Athens* are all there. The late romances are also well served: *Cymbeline*, *Pericles*, *The Tempest*, and *The Winter's Tale* are all included. But the 'problem plays' are less complete: *All's Well That Ends Well*, *Measure for Measure*, and *The Merchant of Venice* are included while *Troilus and Cressida* is missing. The

English histories are notable by their complete absence: there is no *King John*; no *Richard II, Henry IV, Parts 1* or *2*, and no *Henry V*; no *Henry VI, Parts 1, 2* or *3*; no *Richard III*; and no *Henry VIII*. The Roman tales—*Antony and Cleopatra*, *Coriolanus*, and *Julius Caesar*—are nowhere to be found. *Titus Andronicus*—a hybrid that is part tragedy and part Roman play—is also missing.

The Lamb *Tales* need to be supplemented, then, by the works of other Shakespearean scholars and enthusiasts. At the forefront stands the figure of Arthur Quiller-Couch, King Edward VII Professor of English Literature at the University of Cambridge and author in his own right, who published his *Historical Tales from Shakespeare* in the early twentieth century. Quiller-Couch was clear about his mission: he was to put into prose those works ('or most of them') that Charles and Mary Lamb had omitted from their *Tales*. Included in his *Historical Tales* are the near-complete English histories, albeit consolidated by reign so that there are no longer separate 'parts' (King John, Richard II, Henry IV, Henry V, Henry VI, and Richard III), as well as two of the Roman tales (*Coriolanus* and *Julius Caesar*). Quiller-Couch took a slightly different approach from the Lambs: he resolved to tell the tales as simply and straightforwardly as he could in his own manner. The result is, for the most part, a great triumph. Quiller-Couch's evocative narration is the perfect adjunct to the intricate and richly textured fabric of

Shakespearean history. Only one difficulty remained: even the Lamb *Tales* and Quiller-Couch's *Historical Tales* taken together leave us with significant omissions. What has happened to *Love's Labour's Lost* and *The Merry Wives of Windsor*? Why have *Antony and Cleopatra* and *Henry VIII* fallen by the wayside? And where are the two 'deplorables' of the Shakespearean universe—the deeply troubling *Troilus and Cressida* and the unspeakably gruesome *Titus Andronicus*?

To complete the tales, then, we need to cross the pond and turn to Harrison Morris and Winston Stokes. Morris, in his own *Tales from Shakespeare*, almost completes the project. Here we find not only the missing comedies, *Love's Labour's Lost* and *The Merry Wives of Windsor*, but also the hitherto absent *Antony and Cleopatra* and *Henry VIII*, as well as the troublesome *Troilus and Cressida*. Morris' new world sensibilities were not yet ready, however, to expose children to the horrors of *Titus Andronicus*. Only Winston Stokes, in *All Shakespeare's Tales*, was able to screw his courage to the sticking place and pen the prose version of this play. Even Stokes, however, wasn't prepared to communicate Shakespeare in his full Renaissance bloodthirstiness: whereas in Stokes' version Lavinia is 'subjected to cruel tortures', in Shakespeare's original she is raped and has her hands lopped off and tongue cut out; and whereas in Stokes' version Andronicus merely 'makes known' to Tamora that he has killed her sons, in the original play he reveals that he has ground their bones and baked their heads in order to make the very pie she has just been eating.

The striking illustrations that accompany the tales are those of Sir John Gilbert. The product of a more meritocratic age than our own, Gilbert was self-taught and immensely prolific. He illustrated Howard Staunton's three-volume edition of *The Works of Shakespeare*, drawing about twenty illustrations for each play (a total of more than 700 pictures). These illustrations are not inserted simply to decorate the tales; they serve also as wayposts and as aide-mémoires. They bring alive to the eye, as the words do to the ear, the inhabitants and occurrences of Shakespeare's worlds. From Puck and the fairies of *A Midsummer Night's Dream* to the witches of *Macbeth* and the storms and shipwrecks of *Pericles* and *The Tempest*, there is a haunting charm in Gilbert's images that supplements and brings out the magic of the Shakespearean tales.

The *Tales* were intended not simply to engage the intellect, enliven the heart, and lift the spirit. Shakespeare's works were also to be, according to the Lambs, 'enrichers of the fancy, strengtheners of virtue, a withdrawing from all selfish and mercenary thoughts, a lesson of all sweet and honourable thoughts and actions, to teach courtesy, benignity, generosity, humanity'. It has become fashionable among privileged circles to mock the idea that literature can elevate us: the Frankfurt School

Marxist Theodor Adorno has, indeed, famously suggested that 'To write poetry after Auschwitz is barbaric'. And yet that same rejection of the higher capacities of the human soul that is exemplified by Adorno (and those like him) is what has led us to where we are today: demoralized by ugliness, materialism, propaganda, and grinding routine. Our hearts cry out for poetry because we are not bugmen; we are wellsprings of as yet unknown potentialities waiting to be brought to life. Shakespeare, more than any other writer the world has known, by virtue of the tremendous range of experience that he communicates, is able to open us up to a world of possibility. These *Tales* cannot give you that world in its entirety: only the original plays themselves can do that. But they are the entrance point to it. The threshold is right here and right now. Step across.

Introduction to Shakespearean Tragedy

Shakespeare's tragedies are among the most powerful and profound works of literature that the world has known.

The ancient Greeks, whose works served as a model and an inspiration for Renaissance playwrights of Shakespeare's generation, had understood that the essence of tragedy is representation of action and life. Aristotle famously said that 'plot is character revealed by action', since a man's character is manifested by what he does rather than by what he says, and since it is in our actions that we are happy or the reverse. The great driving force behind the tragic action stems from the hero's *hamartia*, the 'tragic flaw' that manifests itself in a fatal error of judgment, setting in place a process that ineluctably moves towards the hero's downfall. *Hamartia* often emerges as *hubris*—excessive arrogance or pride—that leads to the hero 'overrreaching' himself prior to his precipitous decline. The tragic plot will accordingly move towards *peripeteia*, the reversal of fortune that takes the hero from a state of happiness to a state of misery, and this is usually accompanied by *anagnorisis*, the recognition that this reversal was brought about by the hero's own actions. A successful tragedy delivers to its audience *catharsis*: the purging of the emotions of pity and fear that are aroused through viewing the tragedy.

Tragedy has been said to constitute a manifestation 'of law' or of the metaphysical order—of 'that which has been and must be'. Tragedy is the story a single individual who disturbs a universal balance that, sooner or later, must be righted again through that individual's demise. Tragedy at its best, though, is neither simply the representation of an oppressive fatalistic mechanism intent on grinding its protagonist into dust, nor is it simply the naturalistic working out of the consequences of a morally reprehensible course of action embarked upon freely and without compulsion. Instead, fatalism and free choice coincide in the concept of *hamartia*: *hamartia* is the agency by which the hero visits his fate upon himself so that his character *becomes* his destiny. When Macbeth is told by the witches that he will be king, he could simply have waited to see whether the prediction would come true; instead, by taking matters into his own hands, he brings about the total concurrence of choice and destiny.

We open this volume with the 'star-crossed lovers' of *Romeo and Juliet*, whose biologistic impulsivity puts in process a tragic action that leads to their joint suicides but at the same time provides us with a glimpse of something that will remain forever beyond death. The enigmatic *Hamlet* comes next: here, in the castle of Elsinore, the young Danish prince mulls and broods over the murder of his father and the remarriage of his mother, before his actions give rise to a whirlwind of devastation that brings to an end the world that he has known and loved. *Othello*, the tale of a man who 'loved not wisely but too well', is also a study in the dark arts of misdirection, deceit, and full-fledged psychological warfare; *Timon of Athens*, on the other hand, depicts the fate of a man buoyed up by credit and wound down by usury. In the monumental *King Lear*, the old king watches helplessly as the thin crust of human civilisation is peeled away and he is exposed to the ferocious dog-eat-dog nature of humanity beneath; in *Macbeth*, on the other hand, the eponymous hero is driven by his overvaunting ambition to take a step that puts him on the path towards paranoia and despotism.

The tragedies of Shakespeare make for great, powerful tales. But that is not all. They are the stories of individuals who have dreamed greatly, dared greatly, and suffered greatly. Yet at no stage is there a moment's 'littleness' about them—no triviality, no hypocrisy, no self-deceit. Above all, there is no shrinking from the consequences of their own actions. 'My path has led me here,' each of them seems to say, 'and better if it had not been so. But here I now am and this is me. I now must live and die the man my choices have made me.' When a person is exposed to material like this their world undergoes an expansion. The tragic figures connect us to something bigger than ourselves: to a 'communion with that something beyond which we can see only through them, and which is the source of their strength and their fate alike."[1] They are, it has been said, instruments as well as victims of the divine lightning, and they connect us momentarily to the unfathomable powers of creation and destruction that lie at the very root of existence.

1. Northrop Frye, *Anatomy of Criticism* (Princeton and Oxford: Oxford University Press, 1971), 208.

ROMEO AND JULIET

INTRODUCTION

Everyone knows of Romeo and Juliet as Shakespeare's 'star-crossed' lovers. The tale, in outline, is simple enough: boy meets girl, they fall in love, they are separated by circumstance, a plan is initiated to save the girl from forced marriage, but everything goes horribly wrong when, through miscommunication, one of the lovers mistakenly assumes the other is dead and commits suicide, prompting the other to do the same. It is a paean, so it seems, to true love. But is there more depth to this tale than meets the eye?

In the first place, what is this 'love' of which Shakespeare tells? It is true, of course, that on Romeo's very first appearance he is already stricken by the pangs of love—but towards a woman by the name of Rosaline rather than Juliet, who is at that point unknown to Romeo. In fact, Romeo is in active pursuit of Rosaline when he first meets Juliet at the feast of the Capulets. That same night, however, Romeo courts Juliet at her balcony, where they exchange promises to meet the next day to marry in secret, and by the end of the second day they are in bed together. This is love at its most biologistic: there is none of our modern 'communication', 'soul-mating', or companionship—it is raw, immediate, and totally compelling attraction between the young male and female animal. One striking and much-remarked-upon element of the tale is that the object of Romeo's passion was a mere thirteen years old. It is a myth, however, that women would marry so early in the Renaissance; eighteen was considered the earliest reasonable age for motherhood, and the average age of marriage for Elizabethan women was twenty-five to twenty-six.[1] Even the playwright's source material had Juliet significantly older than thirteen. Shakespeare was making a point: the strongest passions have their roots in the simplest of biological functions, and nature does not waste time.

The second notable feature of the tale is that its main theme and driving force is not love at all—it's *hate*. The tale opens with violent brawls through the

---

1. J. Karl Franson, 'Too Soon Marr'd: Juliet's Age as Symbol in *Romeo and Juliet*,' *Papers on Language & Literature* 32, no. 3 (1996): 245-246.

streets of Verona between the chief families (really tribes) of Montagues and Capulets—a 'deadly enmity' extending to remotest kindred, followers, and retainers on each side. The ill will deepens and crystallizes when the most aggressive of the young men, Tybalt, sees Romeo and his fellow Montagues attend a feast of the Capulets, and swears vengeance for the intrusion. And the enmity reaches a head when Tybalt abuses Romeo and Mercutio in the streets of Verona, Mercutio reacts, Tybalt kills Mercutio, and Romeo, in turn, kills Tybalt. It has become a cliché to say that 'love trumps hate' but that's not what Shakespeare suggests: in fact, on each occasion in the tale where kindness steps in—where old Lord Capulet forgives Romeo for his uninvited attendance at the feast, or where Romeo attempts to reason with Tybalt—it is frustrated. Love and forbearance are hopeless in the face of hate, for hate simply cannot understand those qualities, and it therefore proceeds to commit its depredations: hate gives rise to further hate, which always prefers to overshoot rather than undershoot, until the hostility has ratcheted up into a state of unbearable tension and all hell breaks loose, resulting in total devastation. Only then, suggests *Romeo and Juliet*, do blood-sworn enemies come together.

Of course, generations of readers and playgoers have found *Romeo and Juliet* to be, ultimately, one of the most uplifting of works, and they come away from it feeling in some way transformed by the experience.

It is in this respect that Shakespeare weaves his unusual magic. What *Romeo and Juliet* does so successfully is to transport us from the reign of *quantity* to the reign of *quality*. The tale presents to us the moment at which a particular attachment renders all other attachments totally irrelevant: a hundred Rosalines could not—to Romeo at least—compare to one Juliet. It condenses all time into the space of one day, and renders that one day worth the experience of all time. And it converts two fallible human beings into almost mythical archetypes whose significance far transcends their time and place. For twenty-first century men and women, caught up in the ever-accelerating pressure to increase the sheer *number* of things—hours worked, dollars earned, gadgets produced, years lived—this kind of reorientation has the most profound of consequences, and is capable of connecting us once again to the true ground of being.

ROMEO AND JULIET

The two chief families in Verona were the rich
Capulets and the Montagues. There had been an old
quarrel between these families, which was grown to
such a height, and so deadly was the enmity between
them, that it extended to the remotest kindred, to
the followers and retainers of both sides, insomuch
that a servant of the house of Montague could not
meet a servant of the house of Capulet, nor a Capulet
encounter with a Montague by chance, but fierce
words and sometimes bloodshed ensued; and
frequent were the brawls from such accidental

meetings, which disturbed the happy quiet of Verona's streets.

Old Lord Capulet made a great supper, to which many fair ladies and many noble guests were invited. All the admired beauties of Verona were present, and all comers were made welcome if they were not of the house of Montague. At this feast of Capulets, Rosaline, beloved of Romeo, son to the old Lord Montague, was present; and though it was dangerous for a Montague to be seen in this assembly, yet Benvolio, a friend of Romeo, persuaded the young lord to go to this assembly in the disguise of a mask, that he might see his Rosaline, and seeing her compare her with some choice beauties of Verona, who (he said) would make him think his swan a crow. Romeo had small faith in Benvolio's words; nevertheless, for the love of Rosaline, he was persuaded to go. For Romeo was a sincere and passionate lover, and one that lost his sleep for love, and fled society to be alone, thinking on Rosaline, who disdained him, and never requited his love with the least show of courtesy or affection; and Benvolio wished to cure his friend of this love by showing him diversity of ladies and company. To this feast of Capulets then young Romeo with Benvolio and their friend Mercutio went masked. Old Capulet bid them welcome, and told them that ladies who had their toes unplagued with corns would dance with them. And the old man was light-hearted and merry, and said that he had worn a mask when he was young, and could have told a whispering tale in a fair lady's ear. And they fell to dancing, and Romeo was suddenly struck with the exceeding beauty of a lady who danced there, who seemed to him to teach the torches to burn bright, and her beauty to show by night like a rich jewel worn by a blackamoor; beauty too rich for use, too dear for earth! like a snowy dove trooping with crows (he said), so richly did her beauty and perfections shine above the ladies her companions. While he uttered these praises, he was overheard by Tybalt, a nephew of Lord Capulet, who knew him by his voice to be Romeo. And this Tybalt, being of a fiery and passionate temper, could not endure that a Montague should come under cover of a mask, to fleer and scorn (as he said) at their solemnities. And he stormed and raged exceedingly, and would have struck young Romeo dead. But his uncle, the old Lord

Capulet, would not suffer him to do any injury at that time, both out of respect to his guests, and because Romeo had borne himself like a gentleman, and all tongues in Verona bragged of him to be a virtuous and well-governed youth. Tybalt, forced to be patient against his will, restrained himself, but swore that this vile Montague should at another time dearly pay for his intrusion.

The dancing being done, Romeo watched the place where the lady stood; and under favour of his masking habit, which might seem to excuse in part the liberty, he presumed in the gentlest manner to take her by the hand, calling it a shrine, which if he profaned by touching it, he was a blushing pilgrim, and would kiss it for atonement.

'Good pilgrim,' answered the lady, 'your devotion shows by far too mannerly and too courtly: saints have hands, which pilgrims may touch, but kiss not.' 'Have not saints lips, and pilgrims too?' said Romeo. 'Ay,' said the lady, 'lips which they must use in prayer.' 'O then, my dear saint,' said Romeo, 'hear my prayer, and grant it, lest I despair.' In such like allusions and loving conceits they were engaged, when the lady was called away to her mother. And Romeo inquiring who her mother was, discovered that the lady whose peerless beauty he was so much struck with was young Juliet, daughter and heir to the Lord Capulet, the great enemy of the Montagues; and that he had unknowingly engaged his heart to his foe. This troubled him, but it could not dissuade him from loving. As little rest had Juliet, when she found that the gentleman that she had been talking with was Romeo and a Montague, for she had been suddenly smit with the same hasty and inconsiderate passion for Romeo which he had conceived for her; and a prodigious birth of love it seemed to her that she must love her enemy, and that her affections should settle there, where family considerations should induce her chiefly to hate.

It being midnight, Romeo with his companions departed; but they soon missed him, for, unable to stay away from the house where he had left his heart, he leaped the wall of an orchard which was at the back of Juliet's house. Here he had not been long, ruminating on his new love, when Juliet appeared above at a window, through which her exceeding beauty seemed to break like the light of the sun in the east; and the moon, which shone in the orchard with a faint light, appeared to Romeo as if sick and pale with grief at the superior lustre of this new sun. And she leaning her cheek upon her hand, he passionately wished himself a glove upon that hand, that he might touch her cheek. She all this while thinking herself alone, fetched a deep sigh, and exclaimed: 'Ah me!' Romeo, enraptured to hear her speak, said softly, and unheard by her: 'O speak again, bright angel, for such you appear, being over my head, like a winged messenger from heaven whom mortals fall back to gaze upon.' She, unconscious of being overheard, and full of the new passion which that night's adventure had given birth to, called upon her lover by name (whom she supposed absent): 'O Romeo, Romeo!' said she, 'wherefore art thou Romeo? Deny thy father, and refuse thy name, for my sake; or if thou wilt not, be but my sworn love, and I no longer will be a Capulet.' Romeo, having this encouragement, would fain have spoken, but he was desirous of hearing more; and the lady continued her passionate discourse with herself (as she thought), still chiding Romeo for being Romeo and a Montague, and wishing him some other name, or that he would put away that hated name, and for that name which was no part of himself, he should take all herself. At this loving word Romeo could no longer refrain, but taking up the dialogue as if her words had been addressed to him personally, and not merely in fancy, he bade her call him Love, or by whatever other name she pleased, for he was no longer Romeo if that name was displeasing to her. Juliet, alarmed to hear a man's voice in the garden, did not at first know who it was that by favour of the night and darkness had thus stumbled upon the discovery of her secret; but when he spoke again, though her ears had not yet drunk a hundred words of that tongue's uttering, yet so nice is a lover's hearing that she immediately knew him to be young Romeo, and she expostulated with him on the danger to which he had exposed himself by climbing the orchard walls, for if any of her kinsmen should find him there, it would be death to him, being a Montague. 'Alack,' said Romeo, 'there is more peril in your eye, than in twenty of their swords. Do you but look kind upon me, lady, and I am proof against their enmity. Better my life should be ended by their hate, than that hated life should be prolonged to live without your love.' 'How came you into this place,' said Juliet, 'and by whose direction?' 'Love directed me,' answered Romeo: 'I am no pilot, yet wert thou as far apart from me as that vast shore which is washed with the farthest sea, I should venture for such merchandise.' A crimson blush came over Juliet's face, yet unseen by Romeo by reason of the night, when she reflected upon the discovery which she had made, yet not meaning to make it, of her love to Romeo. She would fain have recalled her words, but that was impossible: fain would she have stood upon form, and have kept her lover at a distance, as the custom of discreet ladies is, to frown and be perverse, and give their suitors harsh denials at first; to stand off, and affect a coyness or indifference where they most love, that their lovers may not think them too lightly or too easily won; for the difficulty of attainment increases the value of the object. But there was no room in her case for denials, or puttings off, or any of the customary arts of delay and protracted courtship. Romeo had heard from her own tongue, when she did not dream that he was near her, a confession of her love. So with an honest frankness, which the novelty of her situation excused, she confirmed the truth of what he had before heard, and addressing him by the name of fair Montague (love can sweeten a sour name), she begged him not to impute her easy yielding to levity or an unworthy mind, but that he must lay the fault of it (if it were a fault) upon the accident of the night which had so strangely discovered her thoughts. And she added, that though her behaviour to him might not be sufficiently prudent, measured by the custom of her sex, yet that she would prove more true than many whose prudence was dissembling, and their modesty artificial cunning.

Romeo was beginning to call the heavens to witness that nothing was farther from his thoughts than to impute a shadow of dishonour to such an honoured lady, when she stopped him, begging him not to swear; for although she joyed in him, yet she had no joy of that night's contract: it was too rash, too unadvised, too sudden. But he being urgent with her to exchange a vow of love with him that night, she said that she already had given him hers before he requested it; meaning, when he overheard her confession; but she would retract what she then bestowed, for the pleasure of giving it again, for her bounty was as infinite as the sea, and her love as deep. From this loving conference she was called away by her nurse, who slept with her, and thought it time for her to be in bed, for it was near to daybreak; but hastily returning, she said three or four words more to Romeo, the purport of which was that if his love was indeed honourable, and his purpose marriage, she would send a messenger to him tomorrow to appoint a time for their marriage, when she would lay all her fortunes at his feet, and follow him as her lord through the world. While they were settling this point, Juliet was repeatedly called for by her nurse, and went in and returned, and went and returned again, for she seemed as jealous of Romeo going from her as a young girl of her bird, which she will let hop a little from her hand, and pluck it back with a silken thread; and Romeo was as loath to part as she; for the sweetest music to lovers is the sound of each other's tongues at night. But at last they parted, wishing mutually sweet sleep and rest for that night.

The day was breaking when they parted, and Romeo, who was too full of thoughts of his mistress and that blessed meeting to allow him to sleep, instead of going home, bent his course to a monastery hard by, to find Friar Lawrence. The good friar was already up at his devotions, but seeing young Romeo abroad so early, he conjectured rightly that he had not been abed that night, but that some distemper of youthful affection had kept him waking. He was right in imputing the cause of Romeo's wakefulness to love, but he made a wrong guess at the object, for he thought that his love for Rosaline had kept him waking. But when Romeo revealed his new passion for Juliet, and requested the assistance of the friar to marry them that day, the holy man lifted up his eyes and hands in a sort of wonder at the sudden change in Romeo's affections, for he had been privy to all Romeo's love for Rosaline, and his many complaints of her disdain: and he said, that young men's love lay not truly in their hearts, but in their eyes. But Romeo replying that he himself had often chidden him for doting on Rosaline, who could not love him again, whereas Juliet both loved and was beloved by him, the friar assented in some measure to his reasons; and thinking that a matrimonial alliance between young Juliet and Romeo might happily be the means of making up the long breach between the Capulets and the Montagues; which no one more lamented than this good friar, who was a friend to both the families and had often interposed his mediation to make up the quarrel without effect; partly moved by policy, and partly by his fondness for young Romeo, to whom he could deny nothing, the old man consented to join their hands in marriage.

28

Now was Romeo blessed indeed, and Juliet, who knew his intent from a messenger which she had despatched according to promise, did not fail to be early at the cell of Friar Lawrence, where their hands were joined in holy marriage; the good friar praying the heavens to smile upon that act, and in the union of this young Montague and young Capulet to bury the old strife and long dissensions of their families.

The ceremony being over, Juliet hastened home, where she stayed impatient for the coming of night, at which time Romeo promised to come and meet her in the orchard, where they had met the night before; and the time between seemed as tedious to her as the night before some great festival seems to an impatient child that has got new finery which it may not put on till the morning.

That same day, about noon, Romeo's friends, Benvolio and Mercutio, walking through the streets of Verona, were met by a party of the Capulets with the impetuous Tybalt at their head. This was the same angry Tybalt who would have fought with Romeo at old Lord Capulet's feast. He, seeing Mercutio, accused him bluntly of associating with Romeo, a Montague. Mercutio, who had as much fire and youthful blood in him as Tybalt, replied to this accusation with some sharpness; and in spite of all Benvolio could say to moderate their wrath, a quarrel was beginning when Romeo himself passing that way, the fierce Tybalt turned from Mercutio to Romeo, and gave him the disgraceful appellation of villain. Romeo wished to avoid a quarrel with Tybalt above all men, because he was the kinsman of Juliet, and much beloved by her; besides, this young Montague had never thoroughly entered into the family quarrel, being by nature wise and gentle, and the name of a Capulet, which was his dear lady's name, was now rather a charm to allay resentment, than a watchword to excite fury. So he tried to reason with Tybalt, whom he saluted mildly by the name of good Capulet, as if he, though a Montague, had some secret pleasure in uttering that name: but Tybalt, who hated all Montagues as he hated hell, would hear no reason, but drew his weapon; and Mercutio, who knew not of

Romeo's secret motive for desiring peace with Tybalt, but looked upon his present forbearance as a sort of calm dishonourable submission, with many disdainful words provoked Tybalt to the prosecution of his first quarrel with him; and Tybalt and Mercutio fought, till Mercutio fell, receiving his death's wound while Romeo and Benvolio were vainly endeavouring to part the combatants.

Mercutio being dead, Romeo kept his temper no longer, but returned the scornful appellation of villain which Tybalt had given him; and they fought till Tybalt was slain by Romeo. This deadly broil failing out in the midst of Verona at noonday, the news of it quickly brought a crowd of citizens to the spot, and among them the old lords Capulet and

Montague, with their wives; and soon after arrived the Prince himself, who being related to Mercutio, whom Tybalt had slain, and having had the peace of his government often disturbed by these brawls of Montagues and Capulets, came determined to put the law in strictest force against those who should be found to be offenders. Benvolio, who had been eyewitness to the fray, was commanded by the Prince to relate the origin of it; which he did, keeping as near the truth as he could without injury to Romeo, softening and excusing the part which his friends took in it. Lady Capulet, whose extreme grief for the loss of her kinsman Tybalt made her keep no bounds in her revenge, exhorted the Prince to do strict justice upon his murderer, and to pay no attention to Benvolio's representation, who, being Romeo's friend and a Montague, spoke partially. Thus she pleaded against her new son-in-law, but she knew not yet that he was her son-in-law and Juliet's husband. On the other hand was to be seen Lady Montague pleading for her child's life, and arguing with some justice that Romeo had done nothing worthy of punishment in taking the life of Tybalt, which was already forfeited to the law by his having slain Mercutio. The Prince, unmoved by the passionate exclamations of these women, on a careful examination of the facts pronounced his sentence, and by that sentence Romeo was banished from Verona.

Heavy news to young Juliet, who had been but a few hours a bride, and now by this decree seemed everlastingly divorced! When the tidings reached her, she at first gave way to rage against Romeo, who had slain her dear cousin: she called him a beautiful tyrant, a fiend angelical, a ravenous dove, a lamb with a wolf's nature, a serpent-heart hid with a flowering face, and other like contradictory names, which denoted the struggles in her mind between her love and her resentment: but in the end love got the mastery, and the tears which she shed for grief that Romeo had slain her cousin, turned to drops of joy that her husband lived whom Tybalt would have slain. Then came fresh tears, and they were altogether of grief for Romeo's banishment. That word was more terrible to her than the death of many Tybalts.

Romeo, after the fray, had taken refuge in Friar Lawrence's cell, where he was first made acquainted with the Prince's sentence, which seemed to him far more terrible than death. To him it appeared there was no world out of Verona's walls, no living out of the sight of Juliet. Heaven was there where Juliet lived, and all beyond was purgatory, torture, hell. The good friar would have applied the consolation of philosophy to his griefs: but this frantic young man would hear of none, but like a madman he tore his hair, and threw himself all along upon the ground, as he said, to take the measure of his grave. From this unseemly state he was roused by a message from his dear lady, which a little revived him; and then the friar took the advantage to expostulate with him on the unmanly weakness which he had shown. He had slain

Tybalt, but would he also slay himself, slay his dear lady, who lived but in his life? The noble form of man, he said, was but a shape of wax, when it wanted the courage which should keep it firm. The law had been lenient to him, that instead of death, which he had incurred, had pronounced by the Prince's mouth only banishment. He had slain Tybalt, but Tybalt would have slain him: there was a sort of happiness in that. Juliet was alive, and (beyond all hope) had become his dear wife; therein he was most happy. All these blessings, as the friar made them out to be, did Romeo put from him like a sullen misbehaved wench. And the friar bade him beware, for such as despaired (he said) died miserable. Then when Romeo was a little calmed, he counselled him that he should go that night and secretly take his leave of Juliet, and thence proceed straitways to Mantua, at which place he should sojourn, till the friar found fit occasion to publish his marriage, which might be a joyful means of reconciling their families; and then he did not doubt but the Prince would be moved to pardon him, and he would return with twenty times more joy than he went forth with grief. Romeo was convinced by these wise counsels of the friar, and took his leave to go and seek his lady, proposing to stay with her that night, and by daybreak pursue his journey alone to Mantua; to which place the good friar promised to send him letters from time to time, acquainting him with the state of affairs at home.

That night Romeo passed with his dear wife,

gaining secret admission to her chamber from the orchard in which he had heard her confession of love the night before. That had been a night of unmixed joy and rapture; but the pleasures of this night, and the delight which these lovers took in each other's society, were sadly allayed with the prospect of parting, and the fatal adventures of the past day. The unwelcome daybreak seemed to come too soon, and when Juliet heard the morning song of the lark, she would have persuaded herself that it was the nightingale, which sings by night; but it was too truly the lark which sang, and a discordant and unpleasing note it seemed to her; and the streaks of day in the east too certainly pointed out that it was time for these lovers to part. Romeo took his leave of his dear wife with a heavy heart, promising to write to her from Mantua every hour in the day; and when he had descended from her chamber window, as he stood below her on the ground, in that sad foreboding state of mind in which she was, he appeared to her eyes as one dead in the bottom of a tomb. Romeo's mind misgave him in like manner: but now he was forced hastily to depart, for it was death for him to be found within the walls of Verona after daybreak.

This was but the beginning of the tragedy of this pair of star-crossed lovers. Romeo had not been gone many days before the old Lord Capulet proposed a match for Juliet. The husband he had chosen for her, not dreaming that she was married already, was Count Paris, a gallant, young, and noble gentleman, no unworthy suitor to the young Juliet if she had never seen Romeo.

The terrified Juliet was in a sad perplexity at her father's offer. She pleaded her youth unsuitable to marriage, the recent death of Tybalt, which had left her spirits too weak to meet a husband with any face of joy, and how indecorous it would show for the family of the Capulets to be celebrating a nuptial feast, when his funeral solemnities were hardly over: she pleaded every reason against the match, but the true one, namely, that she was married already. But Lord Capulet was deaf to all her excuses, and in a peremptory manner ordered her to get ready, for by the following Thursday she should be married to Paris: and having found her a husband, rich, young, and noble, such as the proudest maid in Verona might joyfully accept, he could not bear that out of an affected coyness, as he construed her denial, she should oppose obstacles to her own good fortune.

In this extremity Juliet applied to the friendly friar, always her counsellor in distress, and he asking her if she had resolution to undertake a desperate remedy, and she answering that she would go into the grave alive rather than marry Paris, her own dear husband living; he directed her to go home, and appear merry, and give her consent to marry Paris, according to her father's desire, and on the next night, which was the night before the marriage, to drink off the contents of a phial which he then gave her, the effect of which would be that for two-and-forty hours after drinking it she should appear cold and lifeless; and when the bridegroom came to fetch her in the morning, he would find her to appearance dead; that then she would be borne, as the manner in that country was, uncovered on a bier, to be buried in the family vault; that if she could put off womanish fear, and consent to this terrible trial, in forty-two hours after swallowing the liquid (such was its certain operation) she would be sure to awake, as from a dream; and before she should awake, he would let her husband know their drift, and he should come in the night, and bear her thence to Mantua. Love, and the dread of marrying Paris, gave young Juliet strength to undertake this horrible adventure; and she took the phial of the friar, promising to observe his directions.

Going from the monastery, she met the young Count Paris, and modestly dissembling, promised to become his bride. This was joyful news to the Lord Capulet and his wife. It seemed to put youth into the old man; and Juliet, who had displeased him exceedingly by her refusal of the Count, was his darling again now she promised to be obedient. All things in the house were in a bustle against the approaching nuptials. No cost was spared to prepare such festival rejoicings as Verona had never before witnessed.

On the Wednesday night Juliet drank off the potion. She had many misgivings lest the friar, to avoid the blame which might be imputed to him for marrying her to Romeo, had given her poison; but then he was always known for a holy man; then lest she should awake before the time that Romeo was to come for her; whether the terror of the place, a vault of dead Capulets' bones, and where Tybalt, all bloody, lay festering in his shroud, would not be enough to drive her distracted; again she thought of all the stories she had heard of spirits haunting the places where their bodies were bestowed. But then her love for Romeo, and her aversion for Paris returned, and she desperately swallowed the draught, and became insensible.

When young Paris came early in the morning with music to awaken his bride, instead of a living Juliet, her chamber presented the dreary spectacle of a lifeless corpse. What death to his hopes! What confusion then reigned through the whole house! Poor Paris lamenting his bride, whom most detestable death had beguiled him of, had divorced from him even before their hands were joined. But still more

piteous it was to hear the mournings of the old Lord
and Lady Capulet, who having but this one, one poor
living child to rejoice and solace in, cruel death had
snatched her from their sight, just as these careful
parents were on the point of seeing her advanced (as
they thought) by a promising and advantageous
match. Now all things that were ordained for the
festival were turned from their properties to do the
office of a black funeral. The wedding cheer served for
a sad burial feast, the bridal hymns were changed for
sullen dirges, the sprightly instruments to melancholy
bells, and the flowers that should have been strewed
in the bride's path, now served but to strew her corse.
Now, instead of a priest to marry her, a priest was
needed to bury her; and she was borne to church
indeed, not to augment the cheerful hopes of the
living, but to swell the dreary numbers of the dead.

Bad news, which always travels faster than good,
now brought the dismal story of his Juliet's death to
Romeo, at Mantua, before the messenger could arrive,
who was sent from Friar Lawrence to apprise him that
these were mock funerals only, and but the shadow
and representation of death, and that his dear lady
lay in the tomb but for a short while, expecting when
Romeo would come to release her from that dreary
mansion. Just before, Romeo had been unusually
joyful and lighthearted. He had dreamed in the night
that he was dead (a strange dream, that gave a dead
man leave to think), and that his lady came and found
him dead, and breathed such life with kisses in his

lips, that he revived, and was an emperor! And now that a messenger came from Verona, he thought surely it was to confirm some good news which his dreams had presaged. But when the contrary to this flattering vision appeared, and that it was his lady who was dead in truth, whom he could not revive by any kisses, he ordered horses to be got ready, for he determined that night to visit Verona, and to see his lady in her tomb. And as mischief is swift to enter into the thoughts of desperate men, he called to mind a poor apothecary, whose shop in Mantua he had lately passed, and from the beggarly appearance of the man, who seemed famished, and the wretched show in his shop of empty boxes ranged on dirty shelves, and other tokens of extreme wretchedness, he had said at the time (perhaps having some misgivings that his own disastrous life might haply meet with a conclusion so desperate), 'If a man were to need poison, which by the law of Mantua it is death to sell, here lives a poor wretch who would sell it him.' These words of his now came into his mind, and he sought out the apothecary, who after some pretended scruples, Romeo offering him gold, which his poverty could not resist, sold him a poison, which, if he swallowed, he told him, if he had the strength of twenty men, would quickly dispatch him.

With this poison he set out for Verona to have a sight of his dear lady in her tomb, meaning, when he had satisfied his sight, to swallow the poison, and be buried by her side. He reached Verona at midnight, and found the churchyard, in the midst of which was situated the ancient tomb of the Capulets. He had provided a light, and a spade, and wrenching iron, and was proceeding to break open the monument, when he was interrupted by a voice, which by the name of *vile Montague*, bade him desist from his unlawful business. It was the young Count Paris, who had come to the tomb of Juliet at that unseasonable time of night, to strew flowers and to weep over the grave of her that should have been his bride. He knew not what an interest Romeo had in the dead, but knowing him to be a Montague, and (as he supposed)

41

a sworn foe to all the Capulets, he judged that he was come by night to do some villainous shame to the dead bodies; therefore in an angry tone he bade him desist; and as a criminal, condemned by the laws of Verona to die if he were found within the walls of the city, he would have apprehended him. Romeo urged Paris to leave him, and warned him by the fate of Tybalt, who lay buried there, not to provoke his anger, or draw down another sin upon his head by forcing him to kill him. But the Count in scorn refused his warning, and laid hands on him as a felon, which Romeo resisting, they fought, and Paris fell. When Romeo, by the help of a light, came to see who it was that he had slain, that it was Paris, who (he learned in his way from Mantua) should have married Juliet, he took the dead youth by the hand, as one whom misfortune had made a companion, and said that he would bury him in a triumphal grave, meaning in Juliet's grave, which he now opened: and there lay his lady, as one whom death had no power upon to change a feature or complexion, in her matchless beauty; or as if Death were amorous, and the lean abhorred monster kept her there for his delight; for she lay yet fresh and blooming, as she had fallen to sleep when she swallowed that benumbing potion; and near her lay Tybalt in his bloody shroud, whom Romeo seeing, begged pardon of his lifeless corpse, and for Juliet's sake called him cousin, and said that he was about to do him a favour by putting his enemy to death. Here Romeo took his last leave of his lady's lips, kissing them; and here he shook the burden of his cross stars from his weary body, swallowing that poison which the apothecary had sold him, whose operation was fatal and real, not like that dissembling potion which Juliet had swallowed, the effect of which was now nearly expiring, and she about to awake to complain that Romeo had not kept his time, or that he had come too soon.

For now the hour was arrived at which the friar had promised that she should awake; and he, having learned that his letters which he had sent to Mantua, by some unlucky detention of the messenger had never reached Romeo, came himself, provided with the pickaxe and lantern, to deliver the lady from her confinement; but he was surprised to find a light already burning in the Capulets' monument, and to see swords and blood near it, and Romeo and Paris lying breathless by the monument.

Before he could entertain a conjecture to imagine how these fatal accidents had fallen out, Juliet awoke out of her trance, and seeing the friar near her, she remembered the place where she was, and the occasion of her being there, and asked for Romeo, but the friar, hearing a noise, bade her come out of that place of death, and of unnatural sleep, for a greater power than they could contradict had thwarted their intents; and being frightened by the noise of people coming, he fled: but when Juliet saw the cup closed in her true love's hand, she guessed that poison had been the cause of his end, and she would have swallowed the dregs if any had been left, and she kissed his still warm lips to try if any poison yet did hang upon them; then hearing a nearer noise of people coming, she quickly unsheathed a dagger which she wore, and stabbing herself died by her true Romeo's side.

The watch by this time had come up to the place. A page belonging to Count Paris, who had witnessed the fight between his master and Romeo, had given the alarm, which had spread among the citizens, who went up and down the streets of Verona confusedly exclaiming, a Paris! a Romeo! a Juliet! as the rumour had imperfectly reached them, till the uproar brought Lord Montague and Lord Capulet out of their beds, with the Prince, to inquire into the causes of the disturbance. The friar had been apprehended by some of the watch, coming from the churchyard, trembling, sighing, and weeping, in a suspicious manner. A great multitude being assembled at the Capulets' monument, the friar was demanded by the Prince to deliver what he knew of these strange and disastrous accidents.

And there, in the presence of the old Lords Montague and Capulet, he faithfully related the story of their children's fatal love, the part he took in promoting their marriage, in the hope in that union to end the long quarrels between their families: how Romeo, there dead, was husband to Juliet; and Juliet, there dead, was Romeo's faithful wife; how before he could find a fit opportunity to divulge their marriage, another match was projected for Juliet, who, to avoid the crime of a second marriage, swallowed the sleeping draught (as he advised), and all thought her dead; how meantime he wrote to Romeo, to come and take her thence when the force of the potion should cease, and by what unfortunate miscarriage of the messenger the letters never reached Romeo; further than this the friar could not follow the story, nor knew more than that coming himself, to deliver Juliet from that place of death, he found the Count Paris and Romeo slain. The remainder of the transactions was supplied by the narration of the page who had seen Paris and Romeo fight, and by the servant who came with Romeo from Verona, to whom this faithful lover had given letters to be delivered to his father in the event of his death, which made good the friar's words, confessing his marriage with Juliet, imploring the forgiveness of his parents, acknowledging the buying of the poison of the poor apothecary, and his intent in coming to the monument, to die, and lie with Juliet. All these circumstances agreed together to clear the friar from any hand he could be supposed to have in these complicated slaughters, further than as the unintended consequences of his own well meant yet too artificial and subtle contrivances.

And the Prince, turning to these old lords, Montague and Capulet, rebuked them for their brutal and irrational enmities, and showed them what a scourge Heaven had laid upon such offences, that it had found means even through the love of their children to punish their unnatural hate. And these old rivals, no longer enemies, agreed to bury their long strife in their children's graves; and Lord Capulet requested Lord Montague to give him his hand, calling him by the name of brother, as if in acknowledgement of the union of their families, by the marriage of the young Capulet and Montague; and saying that Lord Montague's hand (in token of reconcilement) was all he demanded for his daughter's jointure: but Lord Montague said he would give him more, for he would raise her a statue of pure gold, that while Verona kept its name, no figure should be so esteemed for its richness and workmanship as that of the true and faithful Juliet. And Lord Capulet in return said that he would raise another statue to Romeo. So did these poor old lords, when it was too late, strive to outdo each other in mutual courtesies: while so deadly had been their rage and enmity in past times that nothing but the fearful overthrow of their children (poor sacrifices to their quarrels and dissensions) could remove the rooted hates and jealousies of the noble families.

2

HAMLET

INTRODUCTION

Hamlet is all about change: about confronting it, accepting it, becoming it.

We know the story already. On a wintry night in a castle at Elsinore, Denmark, the young Prince Hamlet meets with a ghost claiming to be the spirit of the dead king, Hamlet's father. The ghost appears to confirm Hamlet's suspicions that the old king has been murdered by his brother, Claudius, who thereafter married the king's widow, Hamlet's mother, and ascended the throne—and it asks the young Hamlet to avenge his father's death by killing the usurper. The rest of the tale tells of Hamlet's efforts to establish the truth of what he has heard and then to kill Claudius, which, after much soul-searching and several wrong turns, he manages to do in a stunning finale that also results in his own poisoning and death.

Traditionally much of the interest in the play has been directed at Hamlet's character and motivation. Critics have explored at length whether he is an indecisive procrastinator constantly seeking and finding reasons to postpone taking action, or whether his hesitation is justified given the dubious circumstances of the ghost's appearance and the need to verify its information before proceeding to acts of murder and regicide.

Another approach, however, is to consider what the tale as a whole seeks to convey—what CS Lewis called 'the poetry and the situation'. For Lewis, the subject of *Hamlet* was death: in *Hamlet*, death is situated before us at all times as 'the great mystery', and Hamlet himself is the Everyman whose contemplations 'describe so well a certain spiritual region through which most of us have passed and anyone in his circumstances might be expected to pass'. Hamlet represents 'haunted man—man with his mind on the frontier of two worlds, man unable either quite to reject or quite to admit the supernatural, man struggling to get something done as man has struggled from the beginning, yet incapable of achievement because of his inability to understand either himself or his fellows or the real quality of the universe which has produced him.'[1]

Hamlet is indeed confronted and puzzled by death. Yet death is a manifestation of a still more prevalent aspect of human existence—the inevitability of change. For change is intrinsic in time itself: it is no accident that Chronos (time) is depicted as devouring his own sons. Hamlet is confronted by change from the very beginning and he embodies the human tendency to resist it at all turns. Change takes the form of death—here, the death of Hamlet's father. Change also manifests in the remarriage, within two months of her husband's death, of Hamlet's mother, Gertrude, to the new king. Much of the tale tells of Hamlet's resistance both to the fact of the death and the 'indecent haste' of the remarriage. That is why he stalks the palace at Elsinore in a suit of deep black, as if still mourning his father, even at his mother's wedding day.

Once he accepts both the fact of change and the inevitability of facing up to his life mission, however, Hamlet is able to draw upon tremendous psychological and existential energy. The change happens when Hamlet kills Polonius; the Rubicon has been crossed, and from this point on the tale accelerates towards its explosive finale. Hamlet is dispatched to England to be killed, only to turn the tables on his captors, marking them for execution in his place, and then escaping by boarding a pirate ship to make his way back to Denmark. Ophelia goes mad, having heard that her lover has killed her father, and

1. CS Lewis, 'Hamlet - The Prince or the Poem,' *Proceedings of the British Academy* 28 (London: Humphrey Milford, 1942).

drowns. Hamlet and Ophelia's brother, Laertes, tussle at Ophelia's grave. And then, during the course of the duel, Laertes kills Hamlet, Hamlet kills Laertes, Gertrude is accidentally poisoned, and Hamlet finally kills the usurping king.

One thing, though, is clear. Accepting change in *Hamlet* does not mean passive resignation towards the status quo; it is a call to action—and potentially violent action at that—to defeat corruption and degeneracy that has arisen in the community, and to pave the way for a new regime freed from the elements that stand in the way of a healthy natural order. Hamlet is a figure from our past. But he may well also, then, be a figure for our future.

HAMLET

Gertrude, Queen of Denmark, becoming a widow by the sudden death of King Hamlet, in less than two months after his death married his brother Claudius, which was noted by all people at the time for a strange act of indiscretion, or unfeelingness, or worse: for this Claudius did no ways resemble her late husband in the qualities of his person or his mind, but was as contemptible in outward appearance as he was base and unworthy in disposition; and suspicions did not fail to arise in the minds of some that he had privately made away with his brother, the late king, with the view of marrying his widow, and ascending the throne of Denmark, to the exclusion of young Hamlet, the son of the buried king, and lawful successor to the throne.

But upon no one did this unadvised action of the Queen make such impression as upon this young prince, who loved and venerated the memory of his dead father almost to idolatry, and being of a nice sense of honour, and a most exquisite practiser of propriety himself, did sorely take to heart this unworthy conduct of his mother Gertrude: insomuch that, between grief for his father's death and shame for his mother's marriage, this young prince was overclouded with a deep melancholy, and lost all his mirth and all his good looks; all his customary pleasure in books forsook him, his princely exercises and sports, proper to his youth, were no longer acceptable; he grew weary of the world, which seemed to him an unweeded garden, where all the wholesome flowers were choked up, and nothing but weeds could thrive. Not that the prospect of exclusion from the throne, his lawful inheritance, weighed so much upon his spirits, though that to a young and high-minded prince was a bitter wound and a sore indignity; but what so galled him, and took away all his cheerful spirits, was that his mother had shown herself so forgetful to his father's memory. And such a father—who had been to her so loving and so gentle a husband! And then she always appeared as loving

54

and obedient a wife to him, and would hang upon him as if her affection grew to him: and now within two months, or as it seemed to young Hamlet, less than two months, she had married again, married his uncle, her dear husband's brother, in itself a highly improper and unlawful marriage from the nearness of relationship, but made much more so by the indecent haste with which it was concluded, and the unkingly character of the man whom she had chosen to be the partner of her throne and bed. This it was which more than the loss of ten kingdoms dashed the spirits and brought a cloud over the mind of this honourable young prince.

In vain was all that his mother Gertrude or the King could do to contrive to divert him; he still appeared in court in a suit of deep black, as mourning for the king his father's death, which mode of dress he had never laid aside, not even in compliment to his mother upon the day she was married, nor could he be brought to join in any of the festivities or rejoicings of that (as appeared to him) disgraceful day.

What mostly troubled him was an uncertainty about the manner of his father's death. It was given out by Claudius that a serpent had stung him; but young Hamlet had shrewd suspicions that Claudius himself was the serpent; in plain English, that he had murdered him for his crown, and that the serpent who stung his father did now sit on the throne.

How far he was right in this conjecture, and what he ought to think of his mother, how far she was privy to this murder, and whether by her consent or knowledge, or without, it came to pass, were the doubts which continually harassed and distracted him.

A rumour had reached the ear of young Hamlet, that an apparition, exactly resembling the dead king his father, had been seen by the soldiers upon watch, on the platform before the palace at midnight, for two or three nights successively. The figure came constantly clad in the same suit of armour, from head to foot, which the dead king was known to have worn; and they who saw it (Hamlet's bosom friend Horatio was one) agreed in their testimony as to the time and manner of its appearance: that it came just as the clock struck twelve; that it looked pale, with a face more of sorrow than of anger; that its beard was grisly, and the colour a sable silvered, as they had seen it in his lifetime; that it made no answer when they spoke to it; yet once they thought it lifted up its head, and addressed itself to motion, as if it were about to speak; but in that moment the morning cock crew, and it shrunk in haste away, and vanished out of their sight.

The young prince, strangely amazed at their relation, which was too consistent and agreeing with itself to disbelieve, concluded that it was his father's ghost which they had seen, and determined to take his watch with the soldiers that night, that he might have a chance of seeing it; for he reasoned with himself, that such an appearance did not come for nothing, but that the ghost had something to impart, and though it had been silent hitherto, yet it would speak to him. And he waited with impatience for the coming of night.

When night came he took his stand with Horatio, and Marcellus, one of the guard, upon the platform where this apparition was accustomed to walk; and it being a cold night, and the air unusually raw and nipping, Hamlet and Horatio and their companion fell into some talk about the coldness of the night, which was suddenly broken off by Horatio announcing that the ghost was coming.

At the sight of his father's spirit, Hamlet was struck with a sudden surprise and fear. He at first called upon the angels and heavenly ministers to defend them, for he knew not whether it were a good spirit or bad; whether it came for good or evil; but he gradually assumed more courage; and his father (as it seemed to him) looked upon him so piteously, and as it were desiring to have conversation with him, and did in all respects appear so like himself as he was when he lived, that Hamlet could not help addressing him: he called him by his name, Hamlet, King, Father! and conjured him that he would tell the reason why he had left his grave, where they had seen him quietly bestowed, to come again and visit the earth and the moonlight; and besought him that he would let them know if there was anything which they could do to give peace to his spirit. And the ghost beckoned to Hamlet that he should go with him to some more removed place, where they might be alone; and Horatio and Marcellus would have dissuaded the young prince from following it, for they feared lest it should be some evil spirit, who would tempt him to the neighbouring sea, or to the top of some dreadful cliff, and there put on some horrible shape which might deprive the Prince of his reason. But their counsels and entreaties could not alter Hamlet's determination, who cared too little about life to fear the losing of it; and as to his soul, he said, what could the spirit do to that, being a thing immortal as itself? And he felt as hardy as a lion, and bursting from them, who did all they could to hold him, he followed whithersoever the spirit led him.

And when they were alone together, the spirit broke silence, and told him that he was the ghost of Hamlet, his father, who had been cruelly murdered, and he told the manner of it: that it was done by his own brother Claudius, Hamlet's uncle, as Hamlet had already but too much suspected, for the hope of succeeding to his bed and crown. That as he was sleeping in his garden, his custom always in the afternoon, his treasonous brother stole upon him in his sleep, and poured the juice of poisonous henbane into his ears, which has such an antipathy to the life of man that swift as quicksilver it courses through all the veins of the body, baking up the blood, and spreading a crustlike leprosy all over the skin; thus sleeping, by a brother's hand he was cut off at once from his crown, his queen, and his life; and he adjured Hamlet, if he did ever his dear father love, that he would revenge his foul murder. And the ghost lamented to his son that his mother should so fall off from virtue as to prove false to the wedded love of her first husband, and to marry his murderer; but he cautioned Hamlet, howsoever he proceeded in his revenge against his wicked uncle, by no means to act any violence against the person of his mother, but to leave her to heaven, and to the stings and thorns of conscience. And Hamlet promised to observe the ghost's direction in all things, and the ghost vanished.

And when Hamlet was left alone, he took up a solemn resolution that all he had in his memory, all that he had ever learned by books or observation, should be instantly forgotten by him, and nothing live in his brain but the memory of what the ghost had told him, and enjoined him to do. And Hamlet related the particulars of the conversation which had passed to none but his dear friend Horatio; and he enjoined both to him and Marcellus the strictest secrecy as to what they had seen that night.

The terror which the sight of the ghost had left upon the senses of Hamlet, he being weak and dispirited before, almost unhinged his mind, and drove him beside his reason. And he, fearing that it would continue to have this effect, which might subject him to observation, and set his uncle upon his guard if he suspected that he was meditating anything against him, or that Hamlet really knew more of his father's death than he professed, took up a strange resolution from that time to counterfeit as if he were really and truly mad; thinking that he would be less an object of suspicion when his uncle should believe him incapable of any serious project, and that this real perturbation of mind would be best covered and pass concealed under a disguise of pretended lunacy.

From this time Hamlet affected a certain wildness

and strangeness in his apparel, his speech, and behaviour, and did so excellently counterfeit the madman, that the King and Queen were both deceived, and not thinking his grief for his father's death a sufficient cause to produce such a distemper, for they knew not of the appearance of the ghost, they concluded that his malady was love, and they thought they had found out the object.

Before Hamlet fell into the melancholy way which has been related, he had dearly loved a fair maid called Ophelia, the daughter of Polonius, the King's chief counsellor in affairs of state. He had sent her letters and rings, and made many tenders of his affection to her, and importuned her with love in honourable fashion; and she had given belief to his vows and importunities. But the melancholy which he fell into latterly had made him neglect her, and from the time he conceived the project of counterfeiting madness, he affected to treat her with unkindness, and a sort of rudeness; but she, good lady, rather than reproach him with being false to her, persuaded herself that it was nothing but the disease in his mind, and no settled unkindness, which had made him less observant of her than formerly; and she compared the faculties of his once noble mind and excellent understanding, impaired as they were with the deep melancholy that oppressed him, to sweet bells which in themselves are capable of most exquisite music, but when jangled out of tune, or rudely handled, produce only a harsh and unpleasing sound.

Though the rough business which Hamlet had in hand, the revenging of his father's death upon his murderer, did not suit with the playful state of courtship, or admit of the society of so idle a passion as love now seemed to him, yet it could not hinder but that soft thoughts of his Ophelia would come between, and in one of these moments, when he thought that his treatment of this gentle lady had been unreasonably harsh, he wrote her a letter full of wild starts of passion, and in extravagant terms, such as agreed with his supposed madness, but mixed with some gentle touches of affection, which could not but show to this honoured lady that a deep love for her yet lay at the bottom of his heart. He bade her to doubt the stars were fire, and to doubt that the sun did move, to doubt truth to be a liar, but never to doubt that he loved; with more of such extravagant phrases. This letter Ophelia dutifully showed to her father, and the old man thought himself bound to communicate it to the King and Queen, who from that time supposed that the true cause of Hamlet's madness was love. And the Queen wished that the good beauties of Ophelia might be the happy cause of his wildness, for so she hoped that her virtues might happily restore him to his accustomed way again, to both their honours.

But Hamlet's malady lay deeper than she supposed, or than could be so cured. His father's ghost, which he had seen, still haunted his imagination, and the sacred injunction to revenge his murder gave him no rest till it was accomplished. Every hour of delay seemed to him a sin, and a violation of his father's commands. Yet how to compass the death of the King, surrounded as he constantly was with his guards, was no easy matter. Or if it had been, the presence of the Queen, Hamlet's mother, who was generally with the King, was a restraint upon his purpose, which he could not break through. Besides, the very circumstance that the usurper was his mother's husband filled him with some remorse, and still blunted the edge of his purpose. The mere act of putting a fellow creature to death was in itself odious and terrible to a disposition naturally so gentle as Hamlet's was. His very melancholy, and the dejection of spirits he had so long been in, produced an irresoluteness and wavering of purpose, which kept him from proceeding to extremities. Moreover, he could not help having some scruples upon his mind, whether the spirit which he had seen was indeed his father, or whether it might not be the devil, who he had heard has power to take any form he pleases, and who might have assumed his father's shape only to take advantage of his weakness and his melancholy, to drive him to the doing of so desperate an act as murder. And he determined that he would have more certain grounds to go upon than a vision, or apparition, which might be a delusion.

While he was in this irresolute mind there came to the court certain players, in whom Hamlet formerly used to take delight, and particularly to hear one of them speak a tragical speech describing the death of old Priam, King of Troy, with the grief of Hecuba his queen. Hamlet welcomed his old friends, the players, and remembering how that speech had formerly given him pleasure, requested the player to repeat it; which he did in so lively a manner, setting forth the cruel murder of the feeble old king, with the destruction of his people and city by fire, and the mad grief of the old queen, running barefoot up and down the palace, with a poor clout upon that head where a crown had been, and with nothing but a blanket upon her loins, snatched up in haste, where she had worn a royal robe; that not only it drew tears from all that stood by, who thought they saw the real scene, so lively was it represented, but even the player himself delivered it with a broken voice and real tears. This put Hamlet upon thinking, if that player could so work himself up to passion by a mere fictitious speech to weep for one that he had never seen, for Hecuba, that had been dead so many hundred years, how dull was he, who having a real motive and cue for passion, a real king and a dear father murdered, was yet so little moved, that his revenge all this while had seemed to have slept in dull and muddy forgetfulness! And while he meditated on actors and acting, and the powerful effects which a good play, represented to the life, has upon the spectator, he remembered the instance of some murderer, who seeing a murder on the stage, was by the mere force of the scene and resemblance of circumstances so affected that on the spot he confessed the crime which he had committed. And he determined that these players should play something like the murder of his father before his uncle, and he would watch narrowly what effect it might have upon him, and from his looks he would be able to gather with more certainty if he were the murderer or not. To this effect he ordered a play to be prepared, to the representation of which he invited the King and Queen.

The story of the play was of a murder done in Vienna upon a duke. The duke's name was Gonzago, his wife Baptista. The play showed how one Lucianus, a near relation to the duke, poisoned him in his garden for his estate, and how the murderer in a short time after got the love of Gonzago's wife.

At the representation of this play, the King, who did not know the trap which was laid for him, was present, with his Queen and the whole court, Hamlet sitting attentively near him to observe his looks. The play began with a conversation between Gonzago and his wife, in which the lady made many protestations of love, and of never marrying a second husband, if she should outlive Gonzago; wishing she might be accursed if she ever took a second husband, and adding that no woman did so but those wicked women who kill their first husbands. Hamlet observed the King his uncle change colour at this expression, and that it was as bad as wormwood both to him and to the Queen. But when Lucianus, according to the story, came to poison Gonzago sleeping in the garden, the strong resemblance which it bore to his own wicked act upon the late king, his brother, whom he had poisoned in his garden, so struck upon the conscience of this usurper, that he was unable to sit out the rest of the play, but on a sudden calling for lights to his chamber, and affecting or partly feeling a sudden sickness, he abruptly left the theatre. The King being departed, the play was given over. Now Hamlet had seen enough to be satisfied that the words of the ghost were true, and no illusion; and in a fit of gaiety, like that which comes over a man who suddenly has some great doubt or scruple resolved, he swore to Horatio that he would take the ghost's word for a thousand pounds. But before he could make up his resolution as to what measures of revenge he should take now he was certainly informed that his uncle was his father's murderer, he was sent for by the Queen his mother to a private conference in her closet.

It was by desire of the King that the Queen sent for Hamlet, that she might signify to her son how much his late behaviour had displeased them both, and the King, wishing to know all that passed at that conference, and thinking that the too partial report of a mother might let slip some part of Hamlet's words, which it might much import the King to know, Polonius, the old counsellor of state, was ordered to plant himself behind the hangings in the Queen's closet, where he might unseen hear all that passed.

This artifice was particularly adapted to the disposition of Polonius, who was a man grown old in crooked maxims and policies of state, and delighted to get at the knowledge of matters in an indirect and cunning way.

Hamlet being come to his mother, she began to tax him in the roundest way with his actions and behaviour, and she told him that he had given great offence to his father, meaning the King, his uncle, whom, because he had married her, she called Hamlet's father. Hamlet, sorely indignant that she should give so dear and honoured a name as father seemed to him to a wretch who was indeed no better than the murderer of his true father, with some sharpness replied: 'Mother, you have much offended my father.' The Queen said that was but an idle answer. 'As good as the question deserved,' said Hamlet. The Queen asked him if he had forgotten who it was he was speaking to? 'Alas!' replied Hamlet, 'I wish I could forget. You are the Queen, your husband's brother's wife; and you are my mother: I wish you were not what you are.' 'Nay; then,' said the Queen, 'if you show me so little respect, I will set those to you that can speak,' and was going to send the King or Polonius to him. But Hamlet would not let her go, now he had her alone, till he had tried if his words could not bring her to some sense of her wicked life; and, taking her by the wrist, he held her fast, and made her sit down. She, affrighted at his earnest manner, and fearful lest in his lunacy he should do her a mischief, cried out; and a voice was heard from behind the hangings: 'Help, help, the Queen!' Which Hamlet hearing, and verily thinking that it was the King himself there concealed, he drew his sword and stabbed at the place where the voice came from, as he would have stabbed a rat that ran there, till the voice ceasing, he concluded the person to be dead. But when he dragged for the body, it was not the King, but Polonius, the old officious counsellor, that had planted himself as a spy behind the hangings. 'Oh me!' exclaimed the Queen, 'what a rash and bloody deed have you done!' 'A bloody deed, mother,' replied Hamlet, 'but not so bad as yours, who killed a king, and married his brother.' Hamlet had gone too far to leave off here. He was now in the humour to speak plainly to his mother, and he pursued it. And though the faults of parents are to be tenderly treated by their children, yet in the case of great crimes the son may have leave to speak even to his own mother with some harshness, so as that harshness is meant for her good, and to turn her from her wicked ways, and not done for the purpose of upbraiding. And now this virtuous prince did in moving terms represent to the Queen the heinousness of her offence, in being so forgetful of the dead king, his father, as in so short a space of time to marry with his brother and reputed murderer: such an act as, after the vows which she had sworn to her first husband, was enough to make all vows of women suspected, and all virtue to be accounted hypocrisy, wedding contracts to be less than gamesters' oaths, and religion to be a mockery and a mere form of words. He said she had done such a deed that the heavens blushed at it, and the earth was sick of her because of it. And he showed her two pictures, the one of the late king, her first husband, and the other of the present king, her second husband, and he bade her mark the difference: what a grace was on the brow of his father, how like a god he looked! The curls of Apollo, the forehead of Jupiter, the eye of Mars, and a posture like to Mercury newly alighted on some heaven-kissing hill! This man, he said, had been her husband. And then he showed her whom she had got in his stead: how like a blight or a mildew he looked, for so he had blasted his wholesome brother. And the Queen was sore ashamed that he should so turn her eyes inward upon her soul, which she now saw so black and deformed. And he asked her how she could continue to live with this man, and be a wife to him, who had murdered her first husband, and got the crown by as false means as a thief—and just as he spoke, the ghost of his father, such as he was in his lifetime, and such as he had lately seen it, entered the room, and Hamlet, in great terror, asked what it would have; and the ghost said that it came to remind him of the revenge he had promised, which Hamlet seemed to have forgot; and the ghost bade him speak to his mother, for the grief and terror she was in would else kill her.

It then vanished, and was seen by none but Hamlet, neither could he by pointing to where it stood, or by any description, make his mother perceive it; who was terribly frightened all this while to hear him conversing, as it seemed to her, with nothing; and she imputed it to the disorder of his mind. But Hamlet begged her not to flatter her wicked soul in such a manner as to think that it was his madness, and not her own offences, which had brought his father's spirit again on the earth. And he bade her feel his pulse, how temperately it beat, not like a madman's. And he begged of her with tears to confess herself to heaven for what was past, and for the future to avoid the company of the King, and be no more as a wife to him; and when she should show herself a mother to him, by respecting his father's memory, he would ask a blessing of her as a son. And she promising to observe his directions the conference ended.

And now Hamlet was at leisure to consider who it was that in his unfortunate rashness he had killed; and when he came to see that it was Polonius, the father of the lady Ophelia, whom he so dearly loved, he drew apart the dead body, and, his spirits being now a little quieter, he wept for what he had done.

The unfortunate death of Polonius gave the King a pretence for sending Hamlet out of the kingdom. He would willingly have put him to death, fearing him as dangerous; but he dreaded the people, who loved Hamlet, and the Queen who, with all her faults, doted upon the Prince, her son. So this subtle king, under pretence of providing for Hamlet's safety, that he might not be called to account for Polonius' death, caused him to be conveyed on board a ship bound for

England, under the care of two courtiers, by whom he dispatched letters to the English court, which in that time was in subjection and paid tribute to Denmark, requiring for special reasons there pretended that Hamlet should be put to death as soon as he landed on English ground. Hamlet, suspecting some treachery, in the night-time secretly got at the letters, and skilfully erasing his own name, he in the stead of it put in the names of those two courtiers, who had the charge of him, to be put to death; then sealing up the letters, he put them into their place again. Soon after the ship was attacked by pirates, and a sea-fight commenced; in the course of which Hamlet, desirous to show his valour, with sword in hand singly boarded the enemy's vessel; while his own ship, in a cowardly manner, bore away, and leaving him to his fate, the two courtiers made the best of their way to England, charged with those letters the sense of which Hamlet had altered to their own deserved destruction.

The pirates, who had the Prince in their power, showed themselves gentle enemies; and knowing whom they had got prisoner, in the hope that the Prince might do them a good turn at court in recompense for any favour they might show him, they set Hamlet on shore at the nearest port in Denmark. From that place Hamlet wrote to the King, acquainting him with the strange chance which had brought him back to his own country, and saying that on the next day he should present himself before His

Majesty. When he got home, a sad spectacle offered itself the first thing to his eyes.

This was the funeral of the young and beautiful Ophelia, his once dear mistress. The wits of this young lady had begun to turn ever since her poor father's death. That he should die a violent death, and by the hands of the Prince whom she loved, so affected this tender young maid, that in a little time she grew perfectly distracted, and would go about giving flowers away to the ladies of the court, and saying that they were for her father's burial, singing songs about love and about death, and sometimes such as had no meaning at all, as if she had no memory of what happened to her. There was a willow which grew slanting over a brook, and reflected its leaves on the stream. To this brook she came one day when she was unmatched, with garlands she had been making, mixed up of daisies and nettles, flowers and weeds together, and clambering up to hang her garland upon the boughs of the willow, a bough broke, and precipitated this fair young maid, garland, and all that she had gathered, into the water, where her clothes bore her up for a while, during which she chanted scraps of old tunes, like one insensible to her own distress, or as if she were a creature natural to that element; but long it was not before her garments, heavy with the wet, pulled her in from her melodious singing to a muddy and miserable death. It was the funeral of this fair maid which her brother Laertes was celebrating, the King and Queen and whole court being present, when Hamlet arrived. He knew not what all this show imported, but stood on one side, not inclining to interrupt the ceremony. He saw the flowers strewed upon her grave, as the custom was in maiden burials, which the Queen herself threw in; and as she threw them she said: 'Sweets to the sweet! I thought to have decked thy bride-bed, sweet maid, not to have strewed thy grave. Thou shouldst have been my Hamlet's wife.' And he heard her brother wish that violets might spring from her grave; and he saw him leap into the grave all frantic with grief, and bid the attendants pile mountains of earth upon him, that he might be buried with her. And Hamlet's love for this fair maid came back to him, and he could not bear that a brother should show so much transport of grief, for he thought that he loved Ophelia better than forty thousand brothers. Then discovering himself, he leaped into the grave where Laertes was, all as frantic or more frantic than he, and Laertes knowing him to be Hamlet, who had been the cause of his father's and his sister's death, grappled him by the throat as an enemy, till the attendants parted them; and Hamlet, after the funeral, excused his hasty act in throwing himself into the grave as if to brave Laertes but he said he could not bear that any one should seem to outgo him in grief for the death of the fair Ophelia. And for the time these two noble youths seemed reconciled.

But out of the grief and anger of Laertes for the death of his father and Ophelia, the King, Hamlet's wicked uncle, contrived destruction for Hamlet. He set on Laertes, under cover of peace and reconciliation, to challenge Hamlet to a friendly trial of skill at fencing, which Hamlet accepting, a day was appointed to try the match. At this match all the court was present, and Laertes, by direction of the King, prepared a poisoned weapon. Upon this match great wagers were laid by the courtiers, as both Hamlet and Laertes were known to excel at this sword play; and Hamlet taking up the foils chose one, not at all suspecting the treachery of Laertes, or being careful to examine Laertes' weapon, who, instead of a foil or blunted sword, which the laws of fencing require, made use of one with a point, and poisoned. At first Laertes did but play with Hamlet, and suffered him to gain some advantages, which the dissembling king magnified and extolled beyond measure, drinking to Hamlet's success, and wagering rich bets upon the issue; but after a few passes, Laertes growing warm made a deadly thrust at Hamlet with his poisoned weapon, and gave him a mortal blow. Hamlet incensed, but not knowing the whole of the treachery, in the scuffle exchanged his own innocent weapon for Laertes' deadly one, and with a thrust of Laertes' own sword repaid Laertes home, who was thus justly caught in his own treachery. In this instant the Queen shrieked out that she was poisoned. She had inadvertently drunk out of a bowl which the King had prepared for Hamlet, in case, that being warm in fencing, he should call for drink; into this the treacherous king had infused a deadly poison, to make sure of Hamlet, if Laertes had failed. He had forgotten to warn the Queen of the bowl, which she drank of, and immediately died, exclaiming with her last breath that she was poisoned. Hamlet, suspecting some treachery, ordered the doors to be shut, while he sought it out. Laertes told him to seek no farther, for he was the traitor; and feeling his life go away with the wound which Hamlet had given him, he made confession of the treachery he had used, and now he had fallen a victim to it; and he told Hamlet of the envenomed point, and said that Hamlet had not half an hour to live, for no medicine could cure him; and begging forgiveness of Hamlet, he died, with his last words accusing the King of being the contriver of the mischief. When Hamlet saw his end draw near, there being yet some venom left upon the sword, he suddenly turned upon his false uncle, and thrust the point of it to his heart, fulfilling the promise which he had made to his father's spirit, whose injunction was now accomplished, and his foul murder revenged upon the murderer. Then Hamlet, feeling his breath fail and life departing, turned to his dear friend Horatio, who had been spectator of this fatal tragedy; and with his dying breath requested him that he would live to tell his story to the world (for Horatio had made a motion as if he would slay himself to accompany the Prince in death), and Horatio promised that he would make a true report, as one that was privy to all the circumstances. And, thus satisfied, the noble heart of Hamlet cracked; and Horatio and the bystanders with many tears commended the spirit of this sweet prince to the guardianship of angels. For Hamlet was a loving and a gentle prince, and greatly beloved for his many noble and princelike qualities; and if he had lived, would no doubt have proved a most royal and complete king to Denmark.

3

OTHELLO

INTRODUCTION

Othello is a study in the dark arts of misdirection, deceit, and full-fledged psychological warfare.

The story is simple as it is powerful. Othello, a soldier and general in the service of the Venetian state, has fallen in love with Desdemona, the beautiful young daughter of Brabantio, a rich senator. But Othello is a Moor—a term used to refer to the peoples of North Africa—and Brabantio would naturally expect his daughter to marry a Venetian of senatorial rank. When Brabantio discovers that Othello and Desdemona have gone ahead and got married in private, he is furious, and accuses Othello before the Venetian Senate of using spells and witchcraft to entrap his daughter. Othello defends himself with plain but compelling words, and his account is backed up by that of Desdemona, who loves him with honest simplicity. Brabantio, unable to sustain his plea, reluctantly surrenders his daughter.

The Senate, in any event, has more important matters in hand: the Turks have fitted out a fleet and are preparing for Cyprus, a Venetian stronghold, and Othello is tasked with defending it. No sooner than Othello and Desdemona have arrived in Cyprus, however, but news arrives that the Turkish fleet has already been dispersed by a tempest. It is now that the tragedy picks up pace. For along with Othello has come Iago, an old officer of Othello's who has lately been upstaged by a handsome and accomplished newcomer, Cassio. Iago has 'studied human nature deeply' and he begins to apply this learning to advance his malicious aims. With dark brilliance, he lays the seeds of doubt in Othello's mind as to Desdemona's chastity, and cultivates them with a diabolical care that sends Othello spinning into the depths of jealousy and despair. Convinced of Desdemona's dishonour, Othello murders her, only to have Iago's plot revealed to him shortly afterwards. Othello takes his own life and Iago is surrendered to the law and to 'strict tortures'.

The genius of the tale is in the depiction of Iago and how he goes about his work.

First, Iago *isolates* his target. He arranges for Cassio to get drunk, then sets on some fellow to provoke him, so that a brawl breaks out, swords are drawn, and an officer of Cyprus is injured. Othello, a strict observer of discipline, is compelled to remove Cassio from his post as lieutenant. Iago now has a reason to encourage Cassio to court Desdemona—namely, that she might intercede on his behalf with Othello—and it is this that will serve as the basis for the aspersions that Iago is about to cast on her chastity. But there is more to it than that: from this point on, Othello is isolated and alone, with no friends other than Iago (who is determined to work his downfall) and Desdemona (towards whom he grows increasingly suspicious). Cassio was the very contact with society—and, through society, with reality—that Othello needed.

Next, Iago works to undermine his target's confidence in his own assessments of reality. Othello should not be too jealous but also not 'too secure', says Iago, for Iago knows the dispositions of the Italian ladies, his countrywomen, better than Othello. Furthermore, Othello should not be too confident in his own assessment of Desdemona, suggests Iago, because, after all, she deceived her father, so why should she not deceive her husband? And in marrying a Moor, has not Desdemona shown 'something unnatural in her', and might she not start comparing Othello with other men from her own country? Very little of what Iago says can be challenged; the power of his method is precisely in its raising of questions, each of which leads to a train of thought that conveys Othello deeper and deeper into self-doubt.

Finally, Iago's most diabolical method is that of turning his targets' positive qualities against them.

It is this that disarms them totally. When he wants to entrap Cassio, for example, he plays upon the lieutenant's generous and open temperament (to get him to drink) and his honest admiration for those who deserve respect (to get him to toast and praise Desdemona as a 'most exquisite lady'). When he wants to entrap Desdemona, he plays upon her kindness and pity to get her to intercede with Othello on behalf of Cassio, and so inadvertently feed Othello's jealousy. And when he wants to entrap Othello, he plays upon that very sense of dignity that prevents him from simply asking Desdemona for an explanation.

Othello is a tale about the power of words and the fragility of understanding. It is no accident that Othello wooed Desdemona through storytelling—tales not only of battles, sieges, hairbreadth escapes, vast wildernesses, caverns, and mountains, but also of many wondrous and strange people he has encountered, such as 'cannibals who are man-eaters' and a people 'whose heads do grow beneath their shoulders'. Were these tales true? Or were they true *for Othello*? It is the human condition to create narratives that weave together the disparate strands of our experience in order to make sense of them. Sometimes the stories we tell for ourselves are productive but sometimes they are not. The difficulty for us is that there is no way of knowing, until it is too late, which is which.

OTHELLO

Brabantio, the rich senator of Venice, had a fair daughter, the gentle Desdemona. She was sought to by divers suitors, both on account of her many virtuous qualities, and for her rich expectations. But among the suitors of her own clime and complexion, she saw none whom she could affect: for this noble lady, who regarded the mind more than the features of men, with a singularity rather to be admired than imitated, had chosen for the object of her affections, a Moor, a black, whom her father loved, and often invited to his house.

Neither is Desdemona to be altogether condemned for the unsuitableness of the person whom she selected for her lover. Bating that Othello was black, the noble Moor wanted nothing which might recommend him to the affections of the greatest lady. He was a soldier, and a brave one; and by his conduct in bloody wars against the Turks, had risen to the rank of general in the Venetian service, and was esteemed and trusted by the state.

He had been a traveller, and Desdemona (as is the manner of ladies) loved to hear him tell the story of his adventures, which he would run through from his earliest recollection: the battles, sieges, and encounters, which he had passed through; the perils he had been exposed to by land and by water; his hair-breadth escapes, when he had entered a breach, or marched up to the mouth of a cannon; and how he had been taken prisoner by the insolent enemy, and sold to slavery; how he demeaned himself in that state, and how he escaped; all these accounts, added to the narration of the strange things he had seen in foreign countries: the vast wilderness and romantic caverns, the quarries, the rocks and mountains, whose heads are in the clouds; of the savage nations, the cannibals who are man-eaters, and a race of people in Africa whose heads do grow beneath their shoulders. These travellers' stories would so enchain the attention of Desdemona, that if she were called off at any time by household affairs, she would despatch with all haste that business, and return, and with a greedy ear devour Othello's discourse. And once he took advantage of a pliant hour, and drew from her a prayer that he would tell her the whole story of his life at large, of which she had heard so much but only by parts: to which he consented, and beguiled her of many a tear, when he spoke of some distressful stroke which his youth had suffered.

His story being done, she gave him for his pains a world of sighs: she swore a pretty oath, that it was all passing strange, and pitiful, wondrous pitiful; she wished (she said) she had not heard it, yet she wished that heaven had made her such a man; and then she thanked him, and told him if he had a friend who loved her, he had only to teach him how to tell his story, and that would woo her. Upon this hint, delivered not with more frankness than modesty, accompanied with certain bewitching prettiness, and blushes, which Othello could not but understand, he spoke more openly of his love, and in this golden opportunity gained the consent of the generous lady Desdemona privately to marry him.

Neither Othello's colour nor his fortune were such that it could be hoped Brabantio would accept him for a son-in-law. He had left his daughter free; but he did expect that, as the manner of noble Venetian ladies was, she would choose ere long a husband of senatorial rank or expectations; but in this he was deceived; Desdemona loved the Moor, though he was black, and devoted her heart and fortunes to his valiant parts and qualities. So was her heart subdued to an implicit devotion to the man she had selected for a husband, that his very colour, which to all but this discerning lady would have proved an insurmountable objection, was by her esteemed above all the white skins and clear complexions of the young Venetian nobility, her suitors.

Their marriage, which, though privately carried, could not long be kept a secret, came to the ears of the old man, Brabantio, who appeared in a solemn council of the Senate as an accuser of the Moor Othello, who by spells and witchcraft (he maintained) had seduced the affections of the fair Desdemona to marry him, without the consent of her father, and against the obligations of hospitality.

At this juncture of time it happened that the state of Venice had immediate need of the services of Othello, news having arrived that the Turks with mighty preparation had fitted out a fleet, which was bending its course to the island of Cyprus with intent to regain that strong post from the Venetians, who then held it; in this emergency the state turned its eyes upon Othello, who alone was deemed adequate to conduct the defence of Cyprus against the Turks. So that Othello, now summoned before the Senate, stood in their presence at once as a candidate for a great state employment, and as a culprit, charged with offences which by the laws of Venice were made capital.

The age and senatorial character of old Brabantio commanded a most patient hearing from that grave assembly; but the incensed father conducted his accusation with so much intemperance, producing likelihoods and allegations for proofs, that, when Othello was called upon for his defence, he had only to relate a plain tale of the course of his love; which

he did with such an artless eloquence, recounting the
whole story of his wooing, as we have related it above,
and delivered his speech with so noble a plainness
(the evidence of truth), that the Duke, who sat as chief
judge, could not help confessing that a tale so told
would have won his daughter too; and the spells and
conjurations which Othello had used in his
courtship, plainly appeared to have been no more
than the honest arts of men in love; and the only
witchcraft which he had used, the faculty of telling a
soft tale to win a lady's ear.

This statement of Othello was confirmed by the
testimony of the lady Desdemona herself, who
appeared in court, and professing a duty to her father
for life and education, challenged leave of him to
profess a yet higher duty to her lord and husband,
even so much as her mother had shown in preferring
him (Brabantio) above *her* father.

The old senator, unable to maintain his plea, called
the Moor to him with many expressions of sorrow,
and, as an act of necessity, bestowed upon him his
daughter, whom, if he had been free to withhold her
(he told him), he would with all his heart have kept
from him; adding that he was glad at soul that he
had no other child, for this behaviour of Desdemona
would have taught him to be a tyrant, and hang clogs
on them for her desertion.

This difficulty being got over, Othello, to whom
custom had rendered the hardships of a military life
as natural as food and rest are to other men, readily

undertook the management of the wars in Cyprus; and Desdemona, preferring the honour of her lord (though with danger) before the indulgence of those idle delights in which new-married people usually waste their time, cheerfully consented to his going.

No sooner were Othello and his lady landed in Cyprus than news arrived that a desperate tempest had dispersed the Turkish fleet, and thus the island was secure from any immediate apprehension of an attack. But the war, which Othello was to suffer, was now beginning; and the enemies, which malice stirred up against his innocent lady, proved in their nature more deadly than strangers or infidels.

Among all the general's friends no one possessed the confidence of Othello more entirely than Cassio. Michael Cassio was a young soldier, a Florentine, gay, amorous, and of pleasing address, favourite qualities with women; he was handsome and eloquent, and exactly such a person as might alarm the jealousy of a man advanced in years (as Othello in some measure was), who had married a young and beautiful wife; but Othello was as free from jealousy as he was noble, and as incapable of suspecting as of doing a base action. He had employed this Cassio in his love affair with Desdemona, and Cassio had been a sort of go-between in his suit: for Othello, fearing that himself had not those soft parts of conversation which please ladies, and finding these qualities in his friend, would often depute Cassio to go (as he phrased it) a courting for him: such innocent simplicity being rather an honour than a blemish to the character of the valiant Moor. So that no wonder, if next to Othello himself (but at far distance, as beseems a virtuous wife), the gentle Desdemona loved and trusted Cassio. Nor had the marriage of this couple made any difference in their behaviour to Michael Cassio. He frequented their house, and his free and rattling talk was no unpleasing variety to Othello, who was himself of a more serious temper: for such tempers are observed often to delight in their contraries, as a relief from the oppressive excess of their own; and Desdemona and Cassio would talk and laugh together, as in the days when he went a courting for his friend.

Othello had lately promoted Cassio to be the lieutenant, a place of trust, and nearest to the general's person. This promotion gave great offence to Iago, an older officer who thought he had a better claim than Cassio and would often ridicule Cassio as a fellow fit only for the company of ladies, and one that knew no more of the art of war or how to set an army in array for battle than a girl. Iago hated Cassio, and he hated Othello, as well for favouring Cassio, as for an unjust suspicion, which he had lightly taken up against Othello, that the Moor was too fond of Iago's wife Emilia. From these imaginary provocations, the plotting mind of Iago conceived a horrid scheme of revenge, which should involve both Cassio, the Moor, and Desdemona, in one common ruin.

Iago was artful, and had studied human nature deeply, and he knew that of all the torments which afflict the mind of man (and far beyond bodily torture), the pains of jealousy were the most intolerable, and had the sorest sting. If he could succeed in making Othello jealous of Cassio, he thought it would be an exquisite plot of revenge, and might end in the death of Cassio or Othello, or both; he cared not.

The arrival of the general and his lady in Cyprus, meeting with the news of the dispersion of the enemy's fleet, made a sort of holiday in the island. Everybody gave themselves up to feasting and making merry. Wine flowed in abundance, and cups went round to the health of the black Othello, and his lady the fair Desdemona.

Cassio had the direction of the guard that night, with a charge from Othello to keep the soldiers from excess in drinking, that no brawl might arise to fright the inhabitants, or disgust them with the new-landed forces. That night Iago began his deep-laid plans of mischief: under colour of loyalty and love to the general, he enticed Cassio to make rather too free with the bottle (a great fault in an officer upon guard). Cassio for a time resisted, but he could not long hold out against the honest freedom which Iago knew how to put on, but kept swallowing glass after glass (as Iago still plied him with drink and encouraging songs), and Cassio's tongue ran over in praise of the lady Desdemona, whom he again and again toasted, affirming that she was a most exquisite lady: until at last the enemy which he put into his mouth stole away his brains; and upon some provocation given him by a fellow whom Iago had set on, swords were drawn, and Montano, a worthy officer, who interfered to appease the dispute, was wounded in the scuffle.

The riot now began to be general, and Iago, who had set on foot the mischief, was foremost in spreading the alarm, causing the castle-bell to be rung (as if some dangerous mutiny instead of a slight drunken quarrel had arisen): the alarm-bell ringing awakened Othello, who, dressing in a hurry, and coming to the scene of action, questioned Cassio of the cause. Cassio was now come to himself, the effect of the wine having a little gone off, but was too much ashamed to reply; and Iago, pretending a great reluctance to accuse Cassio, but, as it were, forced into it by Othello, who insisted to know the truth, gave an account of the whole matter (leaving out his own share in it, which Cassio was too far gone to remember) in such a manner, as while he seemed to make Cassio's offence less, did indeed make it appear greater than it was. The result was that Othello, who was a strict observer of discipline, was compelled to take away Cassio's place of lieutenant from him.

Thus did Iago's first artifice succeed completely: he had now undermined his hated rival, and thrust him out of his place; but a further use was hereafter to be made of the adventure of this disastrous night.

Cassio, whom this misfortune had entirely sobered, now lamented to his seeming friend Iago that he should have been such a fool as to transform himself into a beast. He was undone, for how could he ask the general for his place again? He would tell him he was a drunkard. He despised himself. Iago, affecting to make light of it, said that he, or any man living, might be drunk upon occasion; it remained now to make the best of a bad bargain; the general's wife was now the general, and could do anything with Othello; that he were best to apply to the lady Desdemona to mediate for him with her lord; that she was of a frank, obliging disposition, and would readily undertake a good office of this sort, and set Cassio right again in the general's favour; and then this crack in their love would be made stronger than ever. A good advice of Iago, if it had not been given for wicked purposes, which will after appear.

Cassio did as Iago advised him, and made application to the lady Desdemona, who was easy to be won over in any honest suit; and she promised Cassio that she should be his solicitor with her lord, and rather die than give up his cause. This she immediately set about in so earnest and pretty a manner that Othello, who was mortally offended with Cassio, could not put her off. When he pleaded delay, and that it was too soon to pardon such an offender, she would not be beat back, but insisted that it should be the next night, or the morning after, or the next morning to that at farthest. Then she showed how penitent and humbled poor Cassio was, and that his offence did not deserve so sharp a check. And when Othello still hung back: 'What! My lord,' said she, 'that I should have so much to do to plead for Cassio, Michael Cassio, that came a courting for you, and oftentimes, when I have spoken in dispraise of you, has taken your part! I count this but a little thing to ask of you. When I mean to try your love indeed, I shall ask a weighty matter.' Othello could deny nothing to such a pleader, and only requesting that Desdemona would leave the time to him, promised to receive Michael Cassio again in favour.

It happened that Othello and Iago had entered into the room where Desdemona was, just as Cassio, who had been imploring her intercession, was departing at the opposite door; and Iago, who was full of art, said in a low voice, as if to himself, 'I like not that.'

Othello took no great notice of what he said; indeed, the conference which immediately took place with his lady put it out of his head; but he remembered it afterwards. For when Desdemona was gone, Iago, as if for mere satisfaction of his thought, questioned Othello whether Michael Cassio, when Othello was courting his lady, knew of his love. To this the general answering in the affirmative and adding that he had gone between them very often during the courtship, Iago knitted his brow, as if he had got fresh light on some terrible matter, and cried: 'Indeed!' This brought into Othello's mind the words which Iago had let fall upon entering the room, and seeing Cassio with Desdemona; and he began to think there was some meaning in all this: for he deemed Iago to be a just man, and full of love and honesty, and what in a false knave would be tricks, in him seemed to be the natural workings of an honest mind, big with something too great for utterance; and Othello prayed Iago to speak what he knew, and to give his worst thoughts words. 'And what,' said Iago, 'if some thoughts very vile should have intruded into my breast, as where is the palace into which foul things do not enter?' Then Iago went on to say, what a pity it were if any trouble should arise to Othello out of his imperfect observations; that it would not be for Othello's peace to know his thoughts; that people's good names were not to be taken away for slight suspicions; and when Othello's curiosity was raised almost to distraction with these hints and scattered words, Iago, as if in earnest care for Othello's peace of mind, besought him to beware of jealousy: with such art did this villain raise suspicions in the unguarded Othello by the very caution which he pretended to give him against suspicion. 'I know,' said Othello, 'that my wife is fair, loves company and feasting, is free of speech, sings, plays, and dances well; but where virtue is, these qualities are virtuous. I must have proof before I think her dishonest.' Then Iago, as if glad that Othello was slow to believe ill of his lady, frankly declared that he had no proof, but begged Othello to observe her behaviour well when Cassio was by; not to be jealous nor too secure neither, for that he (Iago) knew the dispositions of the Italian ladies, his countrywomen, better than Othello could do; and that in Venice the wives let heaven see many pranks they dared not show their husbands. Then he artfully insinuated that Desdemona deceived her father in marrying with Othello, and carried it so closely, that the poor old man thought that witchcraft had been used. Othello was much moved with this argument, which brought the matter home to him, for if she had deceived her father, why might she not deceive her husband?

Iago begged pardon for having moved him; but Othello, assuming an indifference, while he was really shaken with inward grief at Iago's words, begged him to go on, which Iago did with many apologies, as if unwilling to produce anything against Cassio, whom he called his friend: he then came strongly to the point, and reminded Othello how Desdemona had refused many suitable matches of her own clime and complexion, and had married him, a Moor, which showed unnatural in her, and proved her to have a headstrong will; and when her better judgement returned, how probable it was she should fall upon comparing Othello with the fine forms and clear white complexions of the young Italians her countrymen. He concluded with advising Othello to put off his reconcilement with Cassio a little longer, and in the meanwhile to note with what earnestness Desdemona should intercede in his behalf; for that much would be seen in that. So mischievously did this artful villain lay his plots to turn the gentle qualities of this innocent lady into her destruction, and make a net for her out of her own goodness to entrap her: first setting Cassio on to entreat her mediation, and then out of that very mediation contriving stratagems for her ruin.

The conference ended with Iago's begging Othello to account his wife innocent until he had more decisive proof; and Othello promised to be patient; but from that moment the deceived Othello never tasted content of mind. Poppy, nor the juice of mandragora, nor all the sleeping potions in the world, could ever again restore to him that sweet rest which he had enjoyed but yesterday. His occupation sickened upon him. He no longer took delight in arms. His heart, that used to be roused at the sight of troops, and banners, and battle-array, and would stir and leap at the sound of a drum, or a trumpet, or a neighing war-horse, seemed to have lost all that pride and ambition which are a soldier's virtue; and his military ardour and all his old joys forsook him. Sometimes he thought his wife honest, and at times he thought her not so; sometimes he thought Iago just, and at times he thought him not so; then he would wish that he had never known of it; he was not the worse for her loving Cassio, so long as he knew it not: torn to pieces with these distracting thoughts, he once laid hold on Iago's throat, and demanded proof of Desdemona's guilt, or threatened instant death for his having belied her. Iago, feigning indignation that his honesty should be taken for a vice, asked Othello if he had not sometimes seen a handkerchief spotted with strawberries in his wife's hand. Othello answered that he had given her such a one, and that it was his first gift. 'That same handkerchief,' said Iago, 'did I see Michael Cassio this day wipe his face with.' 'If it be as you say,' said Othello, 'I will not rest till a wide revenge swallow them up: and first, for a token of your fidelity, I expect that Cassio shall be put to death within three days; and for that fair devil (meaning his lady), I will withdraw and devise some swift means of death for her.'

Trifles light as air are to the jealous proofs as strong

as holy writ. A handkerchief of his wife's seen in Cassio's hand was motive enough to the deluded Othello to pass sentence of death upon them both, without once inquiring how Cassio came by it. Desdemona had never given such a present to Cassio, nor would this constant lady have wronged her lord with doing so naughty a thing as giving his presents to another man: both Cassio and Desdemona were innocent of any offence against Othello; but the wicked Iago, whose spirits never slept in contrivance of villainy, had made his wife (a good, but a weak woman) steal this handkerchief from Desdemona, under pretence of getting the work copied, but in reality to drop it in Cassio's way, where he might find it, and give a handle to Iago's suggestion that it was Desdemona's present.

Othello, soon after meeting his wife, pretended that he had a headache (as he might indeed with truth), and desired her to lend him her handkerchief to hold to his temples. She did so. 'Not this,' said Othello, 'but that handkerchief I gave you.' Desdemona had it not about her (for indeed it was stolen, as we have related). 'How?' said Othello, 'this is a fault indeed. That handkerchief an Egyptian woman gave to my mother; the woman was a witch and could read people's thoughts: she told my mother, while she kept it, it would make her amiable, and my father would love her; but, if she lost it, or gave it away, my father's fancy would turn, and he would loathe her as much as he had loved her. She dying gave it to me, and bade me, if I ever married, to give it to my wife. I did so; take heed of it. Make it a darling as precious as your eye.' 'It is possible?' said the frighted lady. ''Tis true,' continued Othello; 'it is a magical handkerchief; a sibyl that had lived in the world two hundred years in a fit of prophetic fury worked it; the silkworms that furnished the silk were hallowed, and it was dyed in a mummy of maidens' hearts conserved.' Desdemona, hearing the wondrous virtues of the handkerchief, was ready to die with fear, for she plainly perceived she had lost it, and with it, she feared, the affections of her husband. Then Othello started, and looked as if he were going to do some rash thing, and still he demanded the handkerchief, which when she could not produce, she tried to divert her husband from too serious thoughts, and cheerfully told him she saw all his talk about the handkerchief was only to put her off from her suit about Michael Cassio, whom she went on to praise (as Iago had foretold), till Othello in perfect distraction burst out of the room, and then Desdemona, though unwillingly, began to suspect that her lord was jealous.

What cause she could have ministered to him she knew not, and then she accused herself for accusing the noble Othello, and thought to be sure that some untoward news from Venice, or some state troubles had muddled his spirits, and made his temper not so sweet as formerly. And she said: 'Men are not gods, and we must not look for that observance from them when they are married, which they show us on the bridal day.' And she beshrewed herself for so unkindly judging of his unkindness.

Again Othello and Desdemona met, and he accused her more plainly of being unfaithful, and of loving another man, but he did not name whom; and Othello wept, and Desdemona said: 'Alas! The heavy day! Why do you weep?' And Othello told her he could have borne all sorts of evils with fortitude—poverty, and disease, and disgrace; but her infidelity had broken his heart; and he called her a weed, that looked so fair, and smelled so sweet, that the sense ached at it; and wished she had never been born. And when he had left her, this innocent lady was so stupefied with wonder at her lord's untrue suspicion of her, that a weight-like sleep came over her, and she only desired her attendant to make her bed, and to lay her wedding-sheets upon it, saying that when people teach their babes, they do it by gentle means and easy tasks, and Othello might have chid her so; for in good faith she was but a child when she was chidden. And this was all the complaint which this gentle lady made.

Desdemona, being retired to bed expecting her lord would follow her, soon fell into a slumber, the effect of her troubled spirits, when Othello entered the chamber, full of the black purpose which he had meditated of putting his lady to death. But when he saw her asleep, he thought he would not shed her blood, nor scar that white skin of hers, more white than alabaster. But he was resolved she should die; else (as he said) she would live to betray more men, as she had done him. Then he kissed her for the last time (as he said), and that kiss was so sweet, that he must needs kiss her again; and he wept, but he said they were cruel tears.

Desdemona was awakened with his kisses, and she looked upon Othello, and she saw him gnaw his under lip, and roll his eyes, and she knew he was always fatal when he looked so; and he bade her prepare for death, and to say her prayers, for he would not kill her soul. And this innocent wife, as she lay at his mercy, begged for compassion, and to know her fault, and then he named Cassio, and the handkerchief which (he said) she had given him; and as the guiltless lady was proceeding to clear herself he suddenly would hear no more, but covering her up in the bed-clothes, stifled her till she died.

In this instant of time was brought into the house Cassio, wounded and bleeding, whom Iago had set one of his creatures on to assassinate; but the fellow not succeeding in his attempt to kill Cassio (whom he wounded, but not mortally), and being himself killed by Iago to prevent discovery, in his pockets were found certain letters, which made the guilt of Iago, and the innocence of Cassio, clear beyond all doubt; and Cassio now came to beg pardon of Othello, and to ask wherein he had offended him that he had employed Iago to murder him.

This discovery was as a thunderstroke to Othello, who now plainly saw that he was no better than a murderer, and that his wife (poor innocent lady) had been ever faithful to him; the extreme anguish of which discovery making life insupportable, he fell upon his sword, and throwing himself upon the body of his dear injured lady, expired.

These rash acts raised much passion of horror and amazement in the bystanders, for Othello had borne a fair reputation, and till he was wrought upon by the arts of a villain, which his own noble nature never gave him leave to suspect, he was a loving and a doting husband. He had loved not wisely, but too well; and his manly eyes (when he learned his mistake), though not used to weep on every small occasion, dropped tears as fast as the Arabian trees their gum. And when he was dead all his former merits and his valiant acts were remembered. Nothing now remained for his successor but to put the utmost censure of the law in force against Iago, who was executed with strict tortures; and to send word to the state of Venice of the lamentable death of their renowned general.

4

KING LEAR

INTRODUCTION

King Lear is often considered Shakespeare's greatest tragedy. It is a monumental work that unpeels, with unrelenting grimness, the thin crust of human civilisation in order to expose the ferocious dog-eat-dog nature of humanity beneath.

The tale begins when the ageing King Lear decides to parcel out his kingdom between his three daughters. He demands to know which of them loves him best so that he can make division accordingly. The two eldest daughters, Goneril and Regan, express their love to him in the most flatteringly effusive terms; Cordelia, on the other hand, disdains such excessive and dishonest flattery, and states only that she loves him as a daughter should. Lear is furious: he disinherits Cordelia, leaving her to marry her one remaining suitor (the King of France), and sends into exile the loyal Earl of Kent for daring to speak up for her. The gravity of Lear's mistake, however, soon becomes obvious. Having stripped himself of his power, he finds that he and his modest retinue are no longer welcome at the households of either Goneril or Regan. With nowhere else to stay, he heads out into the storm, raging madly against the vicious disloyalty of his daughters. Cordelia, informed by Kent of the desperate condition of her father, arrives in Dover with a French army. They are defeated and Cordelia is put to death; Lear and Kent die soon afterwards. Ultimately, the wrongdoers are killed and the Duke of Albany, the husband of Goneril, who has been innocent of what his wife has done, ascends the throne.

One of the great lessons from *Lear* is the danger of overidentifying with one's social role: Lear's downfall is caused by his failure to recognize that the deferential treatment he has received is a result of his position as king rather than his intrinsic nature or qualities. This has grave personal consequences: Lear is unable to see that it is his status and position that induce the shameless flattery of his two eldest daughters, just as he is unable to see that the plain speaking of his youngest daughter is motivated by her desire to communicate with him as father rather than as king. It also has major political and social ramifications: as a king, Lear has been able to command respect, maintain his expansive household and retinue of knights, and govern the realm as he considered fit; he wrongly assumes that having given away his kingdom he will remain able to enjoy similar privileges and treatment. The simple reality is that to maintain such privilege it is necessary to maintain the position that has given rise to it. Disaster awaits those who mythologize their personal esteem into something that exists separately from the raw power that is necessary to enforce it.

King Lear puts in play two opposing conceptions of the 'state of nature'. On the one hand is the conception of a natural order supported by unwritten laws of nature and society that govern political organization, society, and human relations. The alternative conception is the famous Hobbesian 'state of nature' characterised as 'war of every man against every man' such that, in the absence of higher authority, everyone fears and distrusts everyone else, there can be no justice, commerce, or culture, and life is made 'solitary, poor, nasty, brutish, and short'. Adherents of the natural order are Cordelia and Kent; representative of the brutish state of nature are Goneril, Regan, and Edmund. It is clear enough that in *King Lear* destruction is inflicted on all involved precisely because there has been a wholesale descent into the state of nature. While we may, with Shakespeare, prefer to enjoy the fruits of civilized society, it is plain that the brutish state of nature waits in the wings for the moment at which the well-meaning adherents of natural order let down their guard.

King Lear is a tale of immense power. It never lets up: from the moment Lear disinherits Cordelia, we are thrown into a violent storm of human devastation, beginning with the exile of the loyal Kent, proceeding to the rejection and humiliation of Lear by his eldest daughters, through Lear's retreat into the wilderness in the raging storm and his descent into madness, and from there to the failed efforts by Cordelia to reinstate Lear by way of military support brought from France. Even when the tale appears as if it is about to give us a moment's respite, in the reunion of Lear and Cordelia, that is quickly brought to an end by Cordelia's murder and the deaths shortly thereafter of Lear and Kent. This total disintegration arises as a result of the interconnectedness of moral virtues: once one set of duties is disregarded (respect due *to* Lear as both a king and a father as well as respect due *from* Lear to his honest daughter and honest subjects) then performance of other duties (such as loyalty to king, spouses, and siblings) will also tend to fall away in due course. When the forces of good allow the forces of evil to take control, suggests Shakespeare, there can be no possibility of recovery until the old order has collapsed and been totally destroyed, leaving in its place an empty space for a new one to begin.

KING LEAR

Lear, King of Britain, had three daughters: Goneril, wife to the Duke of Albany; Regan, wife to the Duke of Cornwall; and Cordelia, a young maid, for whose love the King of France and Duke of Burgundy were joint suitors, and were at this time making stay for that purpose in the court of Lear.

The old king, worn out with age and the fatigues of government, he being more than fourscore years old, determined to take no further part in state affairs, but to leave the management to younger strengths, that he might have time to prepare for death, which must

113

at no long period ensue. With this intent he called his three daughters to him, to know from their own lips which of them loved him best, that he might part his kingdom among them in such proportions as their affection for him should seem to deserve.

Goneril, the eldest, declared that she loved her father more than words could give out, that he was dearer to her than the light of her own eyes, dearer than life and liberty, with a deal of such professing stuff, which is easy to counterfeit where there is no real love, only a few fine words delivered with confidence being wanted in that case. The King, delighted to hear from her own mouth this assurance of her love, and thinking truly that her heart went with it, in a fit of fatherly fondness bestowed upon her and her husband one-third of his ample kingdom.

Then calling to him his second daughter, he demanded what she had to say. Regan, who was made of the same hollow metal as her sister, was not a whit behind in her profession, but rather declared that what her sister had spoken came short of the love which she professed to bear for his highness; insomuch that she found all other joys dead in comparison with the pleasure which she took in the love of her dear king and father.

Lear blessed himself in having such loving children, as he thought; and could do no less, after the handsome assurances which Regan had made, than bestow a third of his kingdom upon her and her husband, equal in size to that which he had already given away to Goneril.

Then turning to his youngest daughter Cordelia, whom he called his joy, he asked what she had to say, thinking no doubt that she would glad his ears with the same loving speeches which her sisters had uttered, or rather that her expressions would be so much stronger than theirs, as she had always been his darling, and favoured by him above either of them. But Cordelia, disgusted with the flattery of her sisters, whose hearts she knew were far from their lips, and seeing that all their coaxing speeches were only intended to wheedle the old king out of his dominions that they and their husbands might reign in his lifetime, made no other reply but this—that she loved his majesty according to her duty, neither more nor less.

The King, shocked with this appearance of ingratitude in his favourite child, desired her to consider her words, and to mend her speech, lest it should mar her fortunes.

Cordelia then told her father, that he was her father that he had given her breeding, and loved her; that she returned those duties back as was most fit, and did obey him, love him, and most honour him. But that she could not frame her mouth to such large speeches as her sisters had done, or promise to love nothing else in the world. Why had her sisters husbands, if (as they said) they had no love for anything but their father? If she should ever wed, she was sure the lord to whom she gave her hand would want half her love, half of her care and duty; she should never marry like her sisters, to love her father all.

Cordelia, who in earnest loved her old father even almost as extravagantly as her sisters pretended to do, would have plainly told him so at any other time, in more daughter-like and loving terms, and without these qualifications, which did indeed sound a little ungracious; but after the crafty flattering speeches of her sisters, which she had seen draw such extravagant rewards, she thought the handsomest thing she could do was to love and be silent. This put her affection out of suspicion of mercenary ends, and showed that she loved, but not for gain; and that her professions, the less ostentatious they were, had so much the more of truth and sincerity than her sisters'.

This plainness of speech, which Lear called pride, so enraged the old monarch—who in his best of times always showed much of spleen and rashness, and in whom the dotage incident to old age had so clouded over his reason, that he could not discern truth from flattery, nor a gay painted speech from words that came from the heart—that in a fury of resentment he retracted the third part of his kingdom, which yet remained, and which he had reserved for Cordelia, and gave it away from her, sharing it equally between her two sisters and their husbands, the Dukes of Albany and Cornwall; whom he now called to him, and in presence of all his courtiers bestowing a coronet between them, invested them jointly with all the power, revenue, and execution of government, only retaining to himself the name of king; all the rest of royalty he resigned; with this reservation, that himself, with a hundred knights for his attendants, was to be maintained by monthly course in each of his daughters' palaces in turn.

So preposterous a disposal of his kingdom, so little guided by reason, and so much by passion, filled all his courtiers with astonishment and sorrow; but none of them had the courage to interpose between this incensed king and his wrath, except the Earl of Kent, who was beginning to speak a good word for Cordelia, when the passionate Lear on pain of death commanded him to desist; but the good Kent was not so to be repelled. He had been ever loyal to Lear, whom he had honoured as a king, loved as a father, followed as a master; and he had never esteemed his life further than as a pawn to wage against his royal master's enemies, nor feared to lose it when Lear's safety was the motive; nor now that Lear was most his own enemy did this faithful servant of the King forget his old principles, but manfully opposed Lear, to do Lear good; and was unmannerly only because Lear was mad. He had been a most faithful counsellor in times past to the King, and he besought him now that he would see with his eyes (as he had done in many weighty matters), and go by his advice still; and in his best consideration recall this hideous rashness: for he would answer with his life, his judgment that Lear's youngest daughter did not love him least, nor were those empty-hearted whose low sound gave no token of hollowness. When power bowed to flattery, honour was bound to plainness. For Lear's threats, what could he do to him, whose life was already at his service? That should not hinder duty from speaking.

The honest freedom of this good Earl of Kent only stirred up the King's wrath the more, and like a frantic patient who kills his physician, and loves his mortal disease, he banished this true servant, and allotted him but five days to make his preparations for departure; but if on the sixth his hated person was found within the realm of Britain, that moment was to be his death. And Kent bade farewell to the King, and said that since he chose to show himself in such fashion, it was but banishment to stay there; and before he went, he recommended Cordelia to the protection of the gods, the maid who had so rightly thought, and so discreetly spoken; and only wished that her sisters' large speeches might be answered with deeds of love; and then he went, as he said, to shape his old course to a new country.

The King of France and Duke of Burgundy were now called in to hear the determination of Lear about his youngest daughter, and to know whether they would persist in their courtship to Cordelia now that she was under her father's displeasure, and had no fortune but her own person to recommend her; and the Duke of Burgundy declined the match, and would not take her to wife upon such conditions; but the King of France, understanding what the nature of the fault had been which had lost her the love of her father, that it was only a tardiness of speech, and the not being able to frame her tongue to flattery like her sisters, took this young maid by the hand, and saying that her virtues were a dowry above a kingdom, bade Cordelia to take farewell of her sisters and of her father, though he had been unkind, and she should go with him, and be queen of him and of fair France, and reign over fairer possessions than her sisters; and he called the Duke of Burgundy in contempt a waterish duke, because his love for this young maid had in a moment run all away like water.

Then Cordelia with weeping eyes took leave of her sisters, and besought them to love their father well, and make good their professions; and they sullenly told her not to prescribe to them, for they knew their duty; but to strive to content her husband, who had taken her (as they tauntingly expressed it) as Fortune's alms. And Cordelia with a heavy heart departed, for she knew the cunning of her sisters, and she wished her father in better hands than she was about to leave him in.

Cordelia was no sooner gone, than the devilish dispositions of her sisters began to show themselves in their true colours. Even before the expiration of the first month, which Lear was to spend by agreement with his eldest daughter Goneril, the old king began to find out the difference between promises and performances. This wretch having got from her father all that he had to bestow, even to the giving away of the crown from off his head, began to grudge even those small remnants of royalty which the old man had reserved to himself to please his fancy with the idea of being still a king. She could not bear to see him and his hundred knights. Every time she met her father, she put on a frowning countenance; and when the old man wanted to speak with her, she would feign sickness, or anything to get rid of the sight of him; for it was plain that she esteemed his old age a useless burden, and his attendants an unnecessary expense: not only she herself slackened in her expressions of duty to the King, but by her example, and (it is to be feared) not without her private instructions, her very servants affected to treat him with neglect, and would either refuse to obey his orders, or still more contemptuously pretend not to hear them. Lear could not but perceive this alteration in the behaviour of his daughter, but he shut his eyes against it as long as he could, as people commonly are unwilling to believe the unpleasant consequences which their own mistakes and obstinacy have brought upon them.

True love and fidelity are no more to be estranged by ill, than falsehood and hollow-heartedness can be conciliated by good usage. This eminently appears in the instance of the good Earl of Kent, who, though banished by Lear, and his life made forfeit if he were found in Britain, chose to stay and abide all consequences, as long as there was a chance of his being useful to the King his master. See to what mean shifts and disguises poor loyalty is forced to submit sometimes; yet it counts nothing base or unworthy, so as it can but do service where it owes an obligation! In the disguise of a serving man, all his greatness and pomp laid aside, this good Earl proffered his services to the King, who, not knowing him to be Kent in that disguise, but pleased with a certain plainness, or rather bluntness in his answers, which the Earl put on (so different from that smooth oily flattery which he had so much reason to be sick of, having found the effects not answerable in his daughter), a bargain was quickly struck, and Lear took Kent into his service by the name of Caius, as he called himself, never suspecting him to be his once great favourite, the high and mighty Earl of Kent.

This Caius quickly found means to show his fidelity and love to his royal master: for Goneril's steward that same day behaving in a disrespectful manner to Lear, and giving him saucy looks and language, as no doubt he was secretly encouraged to do by his mistress, Caius, not enduring to hear so open an affront put upon his majesty, made no more ado but presently tripped up his heels, and laid the unmannerly slave in the kennel; for which friendly service Lear became more and more attached to him.

Nor was Kent the only friend Lear had. In his degree, and as far as so insignificant a personage could show his love, the poor fool, or jester, that had been of his palace while Lear had a palace, as it was the custom of kings and great personages at that time to keep a fool (as he was called) to make them sport after serious business: this poor fool clung to Lear after he had given away his crown, and by his witty sayings would keep up his good humour, though he could not refrain sometimes from jeering at his master for his imprudence in uncrowning himself, and giving all away to his daughters; at which time, as he rhymingly expressed it, these daughters:

For sudden joy did weep
And he for sorrow sung,
That such a king should play bo-peep
And go the fools among.

And in such wild sayings, and scraps of songs, of which he had plenty, this pleasant honest fool poured out his heart even in the presence of Goneril herself, in many a bitter taunt and jest which cut to the quick: such as comparing the king to the hedge-sparrow, who feeds the young of the cuckoo till they grow old enough, and then has its head bit off for its pains; and saying, that an ass may know when the cart draws the horse (meaning that Lear's daughters, that ought to go behind, now ranked before their father); and that Lear was no longer Lear, but the shadow of Lear; for which free speeches he was once or twice threatened to be whipped.

The coolness and falling off of respect which Lear had begun to perceive were not all which this foolish fond father was to suffer from his unworthy daughter: she now plainly told him that his staying in her palace was inconvenient so long as he insisted upon keeping up an establishment of a hundred knights; that this establishment was useless and expensive, and only served to fill her court with riot and feasting; and she prayed him that he would lessen their number, and keep none but old men about him, such as himself, and fitting his age.

Lear at first could not believe his eyes or ears, nor that it was his daughter who spoke so unkindly. He could not believe that she who had received a crown from him could seek to cut off his train, and grudge him the respect due to his old age. But she persisting in her undutiful demand, the old man's rage was so excited that he called her a detested kite, and said that she spoke an untruth; and so indeed she did, for the hundred knights were all men of choice behaviour and sobriety of manners, skilled in all particulars of duty, and not given to rioting or feasting, as she said. And he bid his horses to be prepared, for he would go to his other daughter, Regan, he and his hundred knights; and he spoke of ingratitude, and said it was a marblehearted devil, and showed more hideous in a child than the sea-monster. And he cursed his eldest daughter Goneril so as was terrible to hear; praying that she might never have a child, or if she had, that it might live to return that scorn and contempt upon her which she had shown to him: that she might feel how sharper than a serpent's tooth it was to have a thankless child. And Goneril's husband, the Duke of Albany, beginning to excuse himself for any share which Lear might suppose he had in the unkindness,

Lear would not hear him out, but in a rage ordered his horses to be saddled, and set out with his followers for the abode of Regan, his other daughter. And Lear thought to himself how small the fault of Cordelia (if it was a fault) now appeared, in comparison with her sister's, and he wept; and then he was ashamed that such a creature as Goneril should have so much power over his manhood as to make him weep.

Regan and her husband were keeping their court in great pomp and state at their palace; and Lear despatched his servant Caius with letters to his daughter, that she might be prepared for his reception, while he and his train followed after. But it seems that Goneril had been beforehand with him, sending letters also to Regan, accusing her father of waywardness and ill humours, and advising her not to receive so great a train as he was bringing with him. This messenger arrived at the same time with Caius, and Caius and he met; and who should it be but Caius's old enemy the steward, whom he had formerly tripped up by the heels for his saucy behaviour to Lear. Caius not liking the fellow's look, and suspecting what he came for, began to revile him, and challenged him to fight, which the fellow refusing, Caius, in a fit of honest passion, beat him soundly, as such a mischief-maker and carrier of wicked messages deserved; which coming to the ears of Regan and her husband, they ordered Caius to be put in the stocks, though he was a messenger from the King her father, and in that character demanded the

highest respect: so that the first thing the King saw
when he entered the castle was his faithful servant
Caius sitting in that disgraceful situation.

This was but a bad omen of the reception which
he was to expect; but a worse followed when, upon
inquiry for his daughter and her husband, he was told
they were weary with travelling all night, and could
not see him; and when lastly, upon his insisting in
a positive and angry manner to see them, they came
to greet him, whom should he see in their company
but the hated Goneril, who had come to tell her own
story, and set her sister against the king her father!

This sight much moved the old man, and still more
to see Regan take her by the hand; and he asked
Goneril if she was not ashamed to look upon his old

white beard. And Regan advised him to go home again with Goneril, and live with her peaceably, dismissing half of his attendants, and to ask her forgiveness; for he was old and wanted discretion, and must be ruled and led by persons that had more discretion than himself. And Lear showed how preposterous that would sound if he were to go down on his knees, and beg of his own daughter for food and raiment, and he argued against such an unnatural dependence, declaring his resolution never to return with her, but to stay where he was with Regan, he and his hundred knights; for he said that she had not forgot the half of the kingdom which he had endowed her with, and that her eyes were not fierce like Goneril's, but mild and kind. And he said that rather than return to Goneril, with half his train cut off, he would go over to France, and beg a wretched pension of the King there, who had married his youngest daughter without a portion.

But he was mistaken in expecting kinder treatment of Regan than he had experienced from her sister Goneril. As if willing to outdo her sister in unfilial behaviour, she declared that she thought fifty knights too many to wait upon him: that five-and-twenty were enough. Then Lear, nigh heart-broken, turned to Goneril and said that he would go back with her, for her fifty doubled five-and-twenty, and so her love was twice as much as Regan's. But Goneril excused herself, and said, what need of so many as five-and-twenty? or even ten? or five? when he might be waited upon by her servants, or her sister's servants? So these two wicked daughters, as if they strove to exceed each other in cruelty to their old father, who had been so good to them, by little and little would have abated him of all his train, all respect (little enough for him that once commanded a kingdom) which was left him to show that he had once been a king! Not that a splendid train is essential to happiness, but from a king to a beggar is a hard change, from commanding millions to be without one attendant; and it was the ingratitude in his daughters' denying it, more than what he would suffer by the want of it, which pierced this poor king to the heart; insomuch that with this double ill-usage, a vexation for having so foolishly given away a kingdom, his wits began to be unsettled, and while he said he knew not what, he vowed revenge against those unnatural hags, and to make examples of them that should be a terror to the earth!

While he was thus idly threatening what his weak arm could never execute, night came on, and a loud storm of thunder and lightning with rain; and his daughters still persisting in their resolution not to admit his followers, he called for his horses, and chose rather to encounter the utmost fury of the storm abroad, than stay under the same roof with these ungrateful daughters; and they, saying that the injuries which wilful men procure to themselves are their just punishment, suffered him to go in that condition and shut their doors upon him.

The winds were high, and the rain and storm increased, when the old man sallied forth to combat with the elements, less sharp than his daughters' unkindness. For many miles about there was scarce a bush; and there upon a heath, exposed to the fury of the storm in a dark night, did King Lear wander out, and defy the winds and the thunder; and he bid the winds to blow the earth into the sea, or swell the waves of the sea till they drowned the earth, that no token might remain of any such ungrateful animal as man. The old king was now left with no other companion than the poor fool, who still abided with him, with his merry conceits striving to outjest misfortune, saying it was but a naughty night to swim in, and truly the king had better go in and ask his daughters' blessing:

But he that has a little tiny wit,
With heigh ho, the wind and the rain!
Must make content with his fortunes fit,
Though the rain it raineth every day.

and swearing it was a brave night to cool a lady's pride.

Thus poorly accompanied, this once great monarch was found by his ever-faithful servant the good Earl of Kent, now transformed to Caius, who ever followed close at his side, though the King did not know him to be the Earl; and he said: 'Alas! Sir, are you here? Creatures that love night, love not such nights as these. This dreadful storm has driven the beasts to their hiding places. Man's nature cannot endure the affliction or the fear.'

And Lear rebuked him and said these lesser evils were not felt where a greater malady was fixed. When the mind is at ease, the body has leisure to be delicate, but the temper in his mind did take all feeling else from his senses, but of that which beat at his heart. And he spoke of filial ingratitude, and said it was all one as if the mouth should tear the hand for lifting food to it; for parents were hands and food and everything to children.

But the good Caius still persisting in his entreaties that the King would not stay out in the open air, at last persuaded him to enter a little wretched hovel which stood upon the heath, where the fool first entering, suddenly ran back terrified, saying that he had seen a spirit. But upon examination this spirit proved to be nothing more than a poor Bedlam beggar, who had crept into this deserted hovel for shelter, and with his talk about devils frighted the fool, one of those poor lunatics who are either mad, or feign to be so, the better to extort charity from the compassionate country people, who go about the country, calling themselves poor Tom and poor Turlygood, saying, 'Who gives anything to poor Tom?', sticking pins and nails and sprigs of rosemary into their arms to make them bleed; and with such horrible actions, partly by prayers, and partly with lunatic curses, they move or terrify the ignorant country folks into giving them alms. This poor fellow was such a one; and the King seeing him in so wretched a plight, with nothing but a blanket about his loins to cover his nakedness, could not be persuaded but that the fellow was some father who had given all away to his daughters, and brought himself to that pass: for nothing he thought could bring a man to such wretchedness but the having unkind daughters.

And from this and many such wild speeches which he uttered, the good Caius plainly perceived that he was not in his perfect mind, but that his daughters' ill usage had really made him go mad. And now the loyalty of this worthy Earl of Kent showed itself in more essential services than he had hitherto found opportunity to perform. For, with the assistance of some of the King's attendants who remained loyal, he had the person of his royal master removed at daybreak to the castle of Dover, where his own friends and influence, as Earl of Kent, chiefly lay; and himself embarking for France, hastened to the court of Cordelia, and did there in such moving terms represent the pitiful condition of her royal father, and set out in such lively colours the inhumanity of her sisters, that this good and loving child with many tears besought the king her husband that he would give her leave to embark for England, with a sufficient power to subdue these cruel daughters and their husbands, and restore the old king her father to his throne; which being granted, she set forth, and with a royal army landed at Dover.

Lear having by some chance escaped from the guardians which the good Earl of Kent had put over him to take care of him in his lunacy, was found by some of Cordelia's train wandering about the fields near Dover, in a pitiable condition, stark mad, and singing aloud to himself with a crown upon his head which he had made of straw, and nettles, and other wild weeds that he had picked up in the cornfields. By the advice of the physicians, Cordelia, though earnestly desirous of seeing her father, was prevailed upon to put off the meeting, till, by sleep and the operation of herbs which they gave him, he should be restored to greater composure. By the aid of these skilful physicians, to whom Cordelia promised all her gold and jewels for the recovery of the old king, Lear was soon in a condition to see his daughter.

A tender sight it was to see the meeting between

this father and daughter: to see the struggles between the joy of this poor old king at beholding again his once darling child, and the shame at receiving such filial kindness from her whom he had cast off for so small a fault in his displeasure; both these passions struggling with the remains of his malady, which in his half crazed brain sometimes made him that he scarce remembered where he was, or who it was that so kindly kissed him and spoke to him; and then he would beg the standers-by not to laugh at him if he were mistaken in thinking this lady to be his daughter Cordelia! And then to see him fall on his knees to beg pardon of his child; and she, good lady, kneeling all the while to ask a blessing of him, and telling him that it did not become him to kneel, but it was her duty, for she was his child, his true and very child Cordelia! And she kissed him (as she said) to kiss away all her sisters' unkindness, and said that they might be ashamed of themselves to turn their old kind father with his white beard out into the cold air, when her enemy's dog, though it had bit her (as she prettily expressed it), should have stayed by her fire such a night as that, and warmed himself. And she told her father how she had come from France with purpose to bring him assistance; and he said that she must forget and forgive, for he was old and foolish, and did not know what he did; but that to be sure she had great cause not to love him, but her sisters had none. And Cordelia said that she had no cause, no more than they had.

So we will leave this old king in the protection of his dutiful and loving child, where, by the help of sleep and medicine, she and her physicians at length succeeded in winding up the untuned and jarring senses which the cruelty of his other daughters had so violently shaken. Let us return to say a word or two about those cruel daughters.

These monsters of ingratitude, who had been so false to their old father, could not be expected to prove more faithful to their own husbands. They soon grew tired of paying even the appearance of duty and affection, and in an open way showed they had fixed their loves upon another. It happened that the object of their guilty loves was the same. It was Edmund, a natural son of the late Earl of Gloucester, who by his treacheries had succeeded in disinheriting his brother Edgar, the lawful heir, from his earldom, and by his wicked practices was now Earl himself; a wicked man, and a fit object for the love of such wicked creatures as Goneril and Regan. It falling out about this time that the Duke of Cornwall, Regan's husband, died, Regan immediately declared her intention of wedding this Earl of Gloucester, which rousing the jealousy of her sister, to whom as well as to Regan this wicked earl had at sundry times professed love, Goneril found means to make away with her sister by poison; but being detected in her practices, and imprisoned by her husband, the Duke of Albany, for this deed, and for her guilty passion for the Earl which had come to his ears, she, in a fit of disappointed love and rage, shortly put an end to her own life. Thus the justice of Heaven at last overtook these wicked daughters.

While the eyes of all men were upon this event, admiring the justice displayed in their deserved deaths, the same eyes were suddenly taken off from this sight to admire at the mysterious ways of the same power in the melancholy fate of the young and virtuous daughter, the lady Cordelia, whose good deeds did seem to deserve a more fortunate conclusion: but it is an awful truth that innocence and piety are not always successful in this world. The forces which Goneril and Regan had sent out under the command of the bad Earl of Gloucester were victorious, and Cordelia, by the practices of this wicked earl, who did not like that any should stand between him and the throne, ended her life in prison. Thus, Heaven took this innocent lady to itself in her young years, after showing her to the world an illustrious example of filial duty. Lear did not long survive this kind child.

Before he died, the good Earl of Kent, who had still attended his old master's steps from the first of his daughters' ill usage to this sad period of his decay, tried to make him understand that it was he who had followed him under the name of Caius; but Lear's care-crazed brain at that time could not comprehend how that could be, or how Kent and Caius could be the same person: so Kent thought it needless to trouble him with explanations at such a time, and Lear soon after expiring, this faithful servant to the King, between age and grief for his old master's vexations, soon followed him to the grave.

How the judgment of Heaven overtook the bad Earl of Gloucester, whose treasons were discovered, and himself slain in single combat with his brother, the lawful earl; and how Goneril's husband, the Duke of Albany, who was innocent of the death of Cordelia, and had never encouraged his lady in her wicked proceedings against her father, ascended the throne of Britain after the death of Lear, is needless here to narrate; Lear and his three daughters being dead, whose adventures alone concern our story.

5

TIMON OF ATHENS

INTRODUCTION

Timon of Athens, one of Shakespeare's most under-appreciated works, is a tale about how we best do good to our fellow men. This matters to us on a personal level: we wish to care for, provision, and on occasion make gifts to our loved ones, friends, and acquaintances. It also matters to us on a societal level: for we must also consider what we do collectively, as a community, to provide for those who make calls upon our charity—both those who are deserving, and those who are less so.

Timon is a lord of Athens and a wealthy man—but in enjoying this wealth he affects a 'humour of liberality' that knows no limits. Wealthy and poor alike flock to his house to enjoy the luxurious feasts he provides for them; poets and painters alike receive his indiscriminate patronage; jewellers, mercers, and tradesman of all descriptions ply their wares and find a willing purchaser in Timon. Abundance reigns—but Timon's honest steward, Flavius, is aware that the household is soon to be spent-up, and in debt, and he attempts to alert his master to the precarious situation. Timon is surprised but unworried: he sends messengers to the lords for whom he has provided so handsomely—Lucius, Lucullus, Sempronius, and Ventidius—in full expectation of their assistance. One by one, however, they decline. Rejected by his friends and pursued by his creditors, Timon throws one last feast. This time, however, he serves his guests only rocks and lukewarm water. Immediately thereafter he leaves Athens to live, naked and like a wild beast, in a cave in the woods. When he accidentally finds a hoard of gold buried in the ground, he offers it to the general Alcibiades to fund his invasion of Athens, bidding him to burn all to the ground and spare neither children nor old men. At the end of the tale, Timon dies offstage, leaving only a tomb near the sea to record for eternity his hatred and rejection of all mankind.

The tale is focussed remorselessly on the figure of Timon as a representative of those who indulge in indiscriminate provisioning and exposes the harm that such indiscriminate provisioning can do.

It is harmful, in the first instance, to the

provisioners themselves. Shakespeare's tale foreshadows modern research showing that unilateral and unconditional giving is unlikely to encourage giving back in return, because in one-off encounters, at least, the receiver is more likely to benefit from defecting from the reciprocal arrangement rather than from returning the favour. Generosity can be the foundation for a sustained relationship only when the giver is willing to withdraw in the absence of reciprocity; unilateral and unconditional generosity—the act of giving irrespective of any return—far from heralding the birth of a utopian society of sharing and love, tends to cultivate and promote the dominance of selfish agents.

Indiscriminate giving is also harmful to its recipients. The difficulty begins with the ambiguous motives of the giver: it arises from what is known as the 'potlatch effect'—a potlatch being a ceremonial festival at which gifts are bestowed on guests in an extravagant and wasteful display of wealth. Like potlatch, indiscriminate gift-giving or provisioning, which takes place irrespective of whether the recipients are deserving, can function as a demonstration of the status and power of the giver or provisioner relative to the recipient, rather than an expression of disinterested altruism. This explains why it can be degrading to be provisioned by others. 'We wish to be self-sustained,' says Ralph Waldo Emerson. 'We sometimes hate the meat which we eat, because there seems something of degrading dependence in living by it.'[1]

Indiscriminate giving is, finally, harmful to the community and society as a whole. Timon's liberality results in a total distortion of his society and a misallocation of its resources. All standards are cast aside in the frittering away of Timon's 'helicopter money': poets only need to dedicate their poems to Timon to ensure a sale; painters wanting to dispose of a picture need only ask Timon's opinion on its merits and he would buy it; mercers and jewellers could unload their merchandise upon Timon 'at any price'. It is no surprise that much of Timon's spending comes neither from his own assets nor the fruits of his own industry but from the 'impatient and clamorous creditors, usurers, extortioners, fierce and intolerable in their demands, pleading bonds, interest, mortgage' who return, in the end, to haunt him.

Shakespeare's genius is to show Timon as he really is: a nasty wretch. Timon's true nature is revealed at the end when he seeks to lay waste to Athens, to kill its old men and children, and not to let the cries of virgins, babes, or mothers, hinder making 'one universal massacre' of the city. Shakespeare expressed sympathy for each of his tragic heroes with the exception of Timon.

Uniquely, *Timon of Athens* speaks to the early

1. Ralph Waldo Emerson, 'Gifts,' in *The Complete Works of Ralph Waldo Emerson: Essays, 2nd Series, Volume 3* (Boston, New York: Houghton Mifflin, 1903-1904), 162.

twenty-first-century situation: it presents a topsy-turvy world of reckless spending, distorted incentives, and brutal (if long-postponed) correctives and retributions. It offers a sobering warning of what may become of us if we remain detached from our moorings for too long. How long is too long? As Timon could affirm, the answer to that question may only become apparent when the cupboard is bare and the creditors are knocking at the door.

TIMON OF ATHENS

Timon, a lord of Athens, in the enjoyment of a princely fortune, affected a humour of liberality which knew no limits. His almost infinite wealth could not flow in so fast, but he poured it out faster upon all sorts and degrees of people. Not the poor only tasted of his bounty, but great lords did not disdain to rank themselves among his dependents and followers. His table was resorted to by all the luxurious feasters, and his house was open to all comers and goers at Athens. His large wealth combined with his free and prodigal nature to subdue all hearts to his love; men of all minds and dispositions tendered their services to Lord Timon, from the glass-faced flatterer, whose face reflects as in a mirror the present humour of his patron, to the rough and unbending cynic, who affecting a contempt of men's persons, and an indifference to worldly things, yet could not stand out against the gracious manners and munificent soul of Lord Timon, but would come (against his nature) to partake of his royal entertainments, and return most rich in his own estimation if he had received a nod or a salutation from Timon.

If a poet had composed a work which wanted a recommendatory introduction to the world, he had no more to do but to dedicate it to Lord Timon, and the poem was sure of sale, besides a present purse from the patron, and daily access to his house and table. If a painter had a picture to dispose of, he had only to take it to Lord Timon, and pretend to consult his taste as to the merits of it; nothing more was wanting to persuade the liberal-hearted lord to buy it. If a jeweller had a stone of price, or a mercer rich costly stuffs, which for their costliness lay upon his hands, Lord Timon's house was a ready mart always open, where they might get off their wares or their jewellery at any price, and the good-natured lord would thank them into the bargain, as if they had done him a piece of courtesy in letting him have the refusal of such precious commodities. So that by this means his house was thronged with superfluous purchases, of no use but to swell uneasy and ostentatious pomp; and his person was still more inconveniently beset with a crowd of these idle visitors, lying poets, painters, sharking tradesmen, lords, ladies, needy courtiers, and expectants, who continually filled his lobbies, raining their fulsome flatteries in whispers in his ears, sacrificing to him with adulation as to a God, making sacred the very stirrup by which he mounted his horse, and seeming as though they drank the free air but through his permission and bounty.

Some of these daily dependents were young men of birth, who (their means not answering to their extravagance) had been put in prison by creditors, and redeemed thence by Lord Timon; these young prodigals thenceforward fastened upon his lordship, as if by common sympathy he were necessarily endeared to all such spendthrifts and loose livers, who, not being able to follow him in his wealth, found it easier to copy him in prodigality and copious spending of what was not their own. One of these flesh-flies was Ventidius, for whose debts, unjustly contracted, Timon but lately had paid down the sum of five talents.

But among this confluence, this great flood of visitors, none were more conspicuous than the makers of presents and givers of gifts. It was fortunate for these men if Timon took a fancy to a dog or a horse, or any piece of cheap furniture which was theirs. The thing so praised, whatever it was, was sure to be sent the next morning with the compliments of the giver for Lord Timon's acceptance, and apologies for the unworthiness of the gift; and this dog or horse, or whatever it might be, did not fail to produce from Timon's bounty, who would not be outdone in gifts, perhaps twenty dogs or horses, certainly presents of far richer worth, as these pretended donors knew well enough, and that their false presents were but the putting out of so much money at large and speedy interest. In this way Lord Lucius had lately sent to Timon a present of four milk-white horses, trapped in silver, which this cunning lord had observed Timon upon some occasion to commend; and another lord, Lucullus, had bestowed upon him in the same pretended way of free gift a brace of greyhounds, whose make and fleetness Timon had been heard to admire; these presents the easyhearted lord accepted without suspicion of the dishonest views of the presenters; and the givers of course were rewarded with some rich return, a diamond or some jewel of twenty times the value of their false and mercenary donation.

Sometimes these creatures would go to work in a more direct way, and with gross and palpable artifice, which yet the credulous Timon was too blind to see, would affect to admire and praise something that Timon possessed, a bargain that he had bought, or some late purchase, which was sure to draw from this yielding and soft-hearted lord a gift of the thing commended, for no service in the world done for it but the easy expense of a little cheap and obvious flattery. In this way Timon but the other day had given to one of these mean lords the bay courser which he himself rode upon, because his lordship had been pleased to say that it was a handsome beast and went well; and Timon knew that no man ever justly praised what he did not wish to possess. For Lord Timon weighed his friends' affection with his own, and so fond was he of bestowing, that he could have dealt kingdoms to these supposed friends, and never have been weary.

Not that Timon's wealth all went to enrich these wicked flatterers; he could do noble and praiseworthy actions; and when a servant of his once loved the daughter of a rich Athenian, but could not hope to obtain her by reason that in wealth and rank the maid was so far above him, Lord Timon freely bestowed upon his servant three Athenian talents, to make his fortune equal with the dowry which the father of the young maid demanded of him who should be her husband. But for the most part, knaves and parasites had the command of his fortune, false friends whom he did not know to be such, but, because they flocked around his person, he thought they must needs love him; and because they smiled and flattered him, he thought surely that his conduct was approved by all the wise and good. And when he was feasting in the midst of all these flatterers and mock friends, when they were eating him up, and draining his fortunes dry with large draughts of richest wines drunk to his health and prosperity, he could not perceive the difference of a friend from a flatterer, but to his deluded eyes (made proud with the sight) it seemed a precious comfort to have so many like brothers commanding one another's fortunes (though it was his own fortune which paid all the costs), and with joy they would run over at the spectacle of such, as it appeared to him, truly festive and fraternal meeting.

But while he thus outwent the very heart of kindness, and poured out his bounty, as if Plutus, the god of gold, had been but his steward; while thus he proceeded without care or stop, so senseless of expense that he would neither inquire how he could maintain it, nor cease his wild flow of riot; his riches, which were not infinite, must needs melt away before a prodigality which knew no limits. But who should tell him so? His flatterers? They had no interest in shutting his eyes. In vain did his honest steward Flavius try to represent to him his condition, laying his accounts before him, begging of him, praying of him, with an importunity that on any other occasion would have been unmannerly in a servant, beseeching him with tears to look into the state of his affairs.

Timon would still put him off, and turn the discourse to something else; for nothing is so deaf to remonstrance as riches turned to poverty, nothing is so unwilling to believe its situation, nothing so incredulous to its own true state, and hard to give credit to a reverse. Often had this good steward, this honest creature, when all the rooms of Timon's great house have been choked up with riotous feeders at his master's cost, when the floors have wept with drunken spilling of wine, and every apartment has blazed with lights and resounded with music and feasting, often had he retired by himself to some solitary spot, and wept faster than the wine ran from the wasteful casks within to see the mad bounty of his lord, and to think, when the means were gone which brought him praises from all sorts of people, how quickly the breath would be gone of which the praise was made; praises won in feasting would be lost in feasting, and at one cloud of winter-showers these flies would disappear.

But now the time was come that Timon could shut his ears no longer to the representations of this faithful steward. Money must be had; and when he ordered Flavius to sell some of his land for that purpose, Flavius informed him, what he had in vain endeavoured at several times before to make him listen to, that most of his land was already sold or forfeited, and that all he possessed at present was not enough to pay the one half of what he owed. Struck with wonder at this presentation, Timon hastily replied: 'My lands extend from Athens to Lacedaemon.' 'O my good lord,' said Flavius, 'the world is but a world, and has bounds; were it all yours to give in a breath, how quickly were it gone!'

151

Timon consoled himself that no villainous bounty had yet come from him, that if he had given his wealth away unwisely, it had not been bestowed to feed his vices, but to cherish his friends; and he made the kindhearted steward (who was weeping) to take comfort in the assurance that his master could never lack means while he had so many noble friends; and this infatuated lord persuaded himself that he had nothing to do but to send and borrow, to use every man's fortune (that had ever tasted his bounty) in this extremity, as freely as his own. Then with a cheerful look, as if confident of the trial, he severally dispatched messengers to Lord Lucius, to Lords Lucullus and Sempronius, men upon whom he had lavished his gifts in past times without measure or moderation; and to Ventidius, whom he had lately released out of prison by paying his debts, and who, by the death of his father, was now come into the possession of an ample fortune, and well enabled to requite Timon's courtesy: to request of Ventidius the return of those five talents which he had paid for him, and of each of those noble lords the loan of fifty talents; nothing doubting that their gratitude would supply his wants (if he needed it) to the amount of five hundred times fifty talents.

Lucullus was the first applied to. This mean lord had been dreaming overnight of a silver basin and cup, and when Timon's servant was announced, his sordid mind suggested to him that this was surely a making out of his dream, and that Timon had sent him such a present: but when he understood the truth of the matter, and that Timon wanted money, the quality of his faint and watery friendship showed itself, for with many protestations he vowed to the servant that he had long foreseen the ruin of his master's affairs, and many a time had he come to dinner to tell him of it, and had come again to supper to try to persuade him to spend less, but he would take no counsel nor warning by his coming; and true it was that he had been a constant attender (as he said) at Timon's feasts, as he had in greater things tasted his bounty; but that he ever came with that intent, or gave good counsel or reproof to Timon, was a base unworthy lie, which he suitably followed up with meanly offering the servant a bribe, to go home to his master and tell him that he had not found Lucullus at home.

As little success had the messenger who was sent to Lord Lucius. This lying lord, who was full of Timon's meat, and enriched almost to bursting with Timon's costly presents, when he found the wind changed, and the fountain of so much bounty suddenly stopped, at first could hardly believe it; but on its being confirmed, he affected great regret that he should not have it in his power to serve Lord Timon, for unfortunately (which was a base falsehood) he had made a great purchase the day before, which had quite disfurnished him of the means at present, the more beast he, he called himself, to put it out of his power to serve so good a friend; and he counted it one of his greatest afflictions that his ability should fail him to pleasure such an honourable gentleman.

Who can call any man friend that dips in the same dish with him? Just of this metal is every flatterer. In the recollection of everybody, Timon had been a father to this Lucius, had kept up his credit with his purse; Timon's money had gone to pay the wages of his servants, to pay the hire of the labourers who had sweat to build the fine houses which Lucius's pride had made necessary to him: yet, oh! the monster which man makes himself when he proves ungrateful! This Lucius now denied to Timon a sum, which, in respect of what Timon had bestowed on him, was less than charitable men afford to beggars.

Sempronius, and every one of these mercenary lords to whom Timon applied in their turn, returned the same evasive answer or direct denial; even

Ventidius, the redeemed and now rich Ventidius, refused to assist him with the loan of those five talents which Timon had not lent but generously given him in his distress.

Now was Timon as much avoided in his poverty as he had been courted and resorted to in his riches. Now the same tongues which had been loudest in his praises, extolling him as bountiful, liberal, and open handed, were not ashamed to censure that very bounty as folly, that liberality as profuseness, though it had shown itself folly in nothing so truly as in the selection of such unworthy creatures as themselves for its objects. Now was Timon's princely mansion forsaken, and become a shunned and hated place, a place for men to pass by, not a place, as formerly, where every passenger must stop and taste of his wine and good cheer; now, instead of being thronged with feasting and tumultuous guests, it was beset with impatient and clamorous creditors, usurers, extortioners, fierce and intolerable in their demands, pleading bonds, interest, mortgages; iron-hearted men that would take no denial nor putting off, that Timon's house was now his jail, which he could not pass, nor go in nor out for them; one demanding his due of fifty talents, another bringing in a bill of five thousand crowns, which if he would tell out his blood by drops, and pay them so, he had not enough in his body to discharge, drop by drop.

In this desperate and irremediable state (as it seemed) of his affairs, the eyes of all men were suddenly surprised at a new and incredible lustre which this setting sun put forth. Once more Lord Timon proclaimed a feast, to which he invited his accustomed guests, lords, ladies, all that was great or fashionable in Athens. Lord Lucius and Lucullus came, Ventidius, Sempronius, and the rest. Who more sorry now than these fawning wretches, when they found (as they thought) that Lord Timon's poverty was all pretence, and had been only to make trial of their loves, to think that they should not have seen through the artifice at the time, and have had the cheap credit of obliging his lordship? Yet who more glad to find the fountain of that noble bounty, which they had thought dried up, still fresh and running? They came dissembling, protesting, expressing deepest sorrow and shame that when his lordship sent to them they should have been so unfortunate as to want the present means to oblige so honourable a friend. But Timon begged them not to give such trifles a thought, for he had altogether forgotten it. And these base fawning lords, though they had denied him money in his adversity, yet could not refuse their presence at this new blaze of his returning prosperity. For the swallow follows not summer more willingly than men of these dispositions follow the good fortunes of the great, nor more willingly leaves winter than these shrink from the first appearance of a reverse; such summer birds are men. But now with music and state the banquet of smoking dishes was served up; and when the guests had a little done admiring whence the bankrupt Timon could find means to furnish so costly a feast, some doubting whether the scene which they saw was real, as scarce trusting their own eyes; at a signal given, the dishes were uncovered, and Timon's drift appeared: instead of those varieties and far-fetched dainties which they expected, that Timon's epicurean table in past times had so liberally presented, now appeared under the covers of these dishes a preparation more suitable to Timon's poverty, nothing but a little smoke and lukewarm water, fit feast for this knot of mouth-friends, whose professions were indeed smoke, and their hearts lukewarm and slippery as the water with which Timon welcomed his astonished guests, bidding them, 'Uncover, dogs, and lap'; and before they could recover their surprise, sprinkling it in their faces, that they might have enough, and throwing dishes and all after them, who now ran huddling out, lords, ladies, with their caps snatched up in haste, a splendid confusion, Timon pursuing them, still calling them what they were, 'smooth smiling parasites, destroyers under the mask of courtesy, affable wolves, meek bears, fools of fortune, feast-friends, time-flies.' They, crowding out to avoid him, left the house more willingly than they had entered it; some losing their gowns and caps, and some their jewels in the hurry, all glad to escape out of the presence of such a mad lord, and from the ridicule of his mock banquet.

This was the last feast which ever Timon made, and in it he took farewell of Athens and the society of men; for, after that, he betook himself to the woods, turning his back upon the hated city and upon all mankind, wishing the walls of that detestable city might sink, and the houses fall upon their owners, wishing all plagues which infest humanity, war, outrage, poverty, diseases, might fasten upon its inhabitants, praying the just gods to confound all Athenians, both young and old, high and low; so wishing, he went to the woods, where he said he should find the unkindest beast much kinder than mankind. He stripped himself naked, that he might retain no fashion of a man, and dug a cave to live in, and lived solitary in the manner of a beast, eating the wild roots, and drinking water, flying from the face of his kind, and choosing rather to herd with wild beasts, as more harmless and friendly than man.

What a change from Lord Timon the rich, Lord Timon the delight of mankind, to Timon the naked, Timon the man-hater! Where were his flatterers now? Where were his attendants and retinue? Would the bleak air, that boisterous servitor, be his chamberlain, to put his shirt on warm? Would those stiff trees, that had outlived the eagle, turn young and airy pages to him, to skip on his errands when he bade them? Would the cool brook, when it was iced with winter, administer to him his warm broths and caudles when sick of an overnight's surfeit? Or would the creatures that lived in those wild woods come and lick his hand and flatter him?

Here on a day, when he was digging for roots, his poor sustenance, his spade struck against something heavy, which proved to be gold, a great heap which some miser had probably buried in a time of alarm, thinking to have come again, and taken it from its prison, but died before the opportunity had arrived, without making any man privy to the concealment;

so it lay, doing neither good nor harm, in the bowels of the earth, its mother, as if it had never come from thence, till the accidental striking of Timon's spade against it once more brought it to light.

Here was a mass of treasure which, if Timon had retained his old mind, was enough to have purchased him friends and flatterers again; but Timon was sick of the false world, and the sight of gold was poisonous to his eyes; and he would have restored it to the earth, but that, thinking of the infinite calamities which by means of gold happen to mankind, how the lucre of it causes robberies, oppression, injustice, briberies, violence, and murder, among men, he had a pleasure in imagining (such a rooted hatred did he bear to his species) that out of this heap, which in digging he had discovered, might arise some mischief to plague mankind.

And some soldiers passing through the woods near
to his cave at that instant, which proved to be a part
of the troops of the Athenian captain Alcibiades, who
upon some disgust taken against the senators of
Athens (the Athenians were ever noted to be a
thankless and ungrateful people, giving disgust to
their generals and best friends), was marching at the
head of the same triumphant army, which he had
formerly headed in their defence, to war against them;
Timon, who liked their business well, bestowed upon
their captain the gold to pay his soldiers, requiring no
other service from him than that he should with his
conquering army lay Athens level with the ground,
and burn, slay, kill all her inhabitants; not sparing the
old men for their white beards, for (he said) they were
usurers, nor the young children for their seeming
innocent smiles, for those (he said) would live, if they
grew up, to be traitors; but to steel his eyes and ears
against any sights or sounds that might awaken

compassion; and not to let the cries of virgins, babes, or mothers hinder him from making one universal massacre of the city, but to confound them all in his conquest; and when he had conquered, he prayed that the gods would confound him also, the conqueror: so thoroughly did Timon hate Athens, Athenians, and all mankind.

While he lived in this forlorn state, leading a life more brutal than human, he was suddenly surprised one day with the appearance of a man standing in an admiring posture at the door of his cave. It was Flavius, the honest steward, whom love and zealous affection to his master had led to seek him out at his wretched dwelling, and to offer his services; and the first sight of his master, the once noble Timon, in that abject condition, naked as he was born, living in the manner of a beast among beasts, looking like his own sad ruins and a monument of decay, so affected this good servant, that he stood speechless, wrapped up in horror, and confounded. And when he found utterance at last to his words, they were so choked with tears, that Timon had much ado to know him again, or to make out who it was that had come (so contrary to the experience he had had of mankind) to offer him service in extremity. And being in the form and shape of a man, he suspected him for a traitor, and his tears for false; but the good servant by so many tokens confirmed the truth of his fidelity, and made it clear that nothing but love and zealous duty to his once dear master had brought him there, that

Timon was forced to confess that the world contained one honest man; yet, being in the shape and form of a man, he could not look upon his man's face without abhorrence, or hear words uttered from his man's lips without loathing; and this singly honest man was forced to depart, because he was a man, and because, with a heart more gentle and compassionate than is usual to man, he bore man's detested form and outward feature.

But greater visitants than a poor steward were about to interrupt the savage quiet of Timon's solitude. For now the day was come when the ungrateful lords of Athens sorely repented the injustice which they had done to the noble Timon. For Alcibiades, like an incensed wild boar, was raging at the walls of their city, and with his hot siege threatened to lay fair Athens in the dust. And now the memory of Lord Timon's former prowess and military conduct came fresh into their forgetful minds, for Timon had been their general in past times, and a valiant and expert soldier, who alone of all the Athenians was deemed able to cope with a besieging army such as then threatened them, or to drive back the furious approaches of Alcibiades.

A deputation of the senators was chosen in this emergency to wait upon Timon. To him they came in their extremity, to whom, when he was in extremity, they had shown but small regard; as if they presumed upon his gratitude whom they had disobliged, and had derived a claim to his courtesy from their own most discourteous and unpiteous treatment.

Now they earnestly beseech him, implore him with tears, to return and save that city, from which their ingratitude had so lately driven him; now they offer him riches, power, dignities, satisfaction for past injuries, and public honours, and the public love; their persons, lives, and fortunes, to be at his disposal, if he will but come back and save them. But Timon the naked, Timon the man-hater, was no longer Lord Timon, the lord of bounty, the flower of valour, their defence in war, their ornament in peace. If Alcibiades killed his countrymen, Timon cared not. If he sacked fair Athens, and slew her old men and her infants, Timon would rejoice. So he told them; and that there was not a knife in the unruly camp which he did not prize above the reverendest throat in Athens.

This was all the answer he vouchsafed to the weeping disappointed senators; only at parting he bade them commend him to his countrymen, and tell them, that to ease them of their griefs and anxieties, and to prevent the consequences of fierce Alcibiades' wrath, there was yet a way left, which he would teach them, for he had yet so much affection left for his dear countrymen as to be willing to do them a kindness before his death. These words a little revived the senators, who hoped that his kindness for their city was returning. Then Timon told them that he had a tree, which grew near his cave, which he should shortly have occasion to cut down, and he invited all his friends in Athens, high or low, of what degree soever, who wished to shun affliction, to come and take a taste of his tree before he cut it down; meaning, that they might come and hang themselves on it, and escape affliction that way.

And this was the last courtesy of all his noble bounties which Timon showed to mankind, and this the last sight of him which his countrymen had: for not many days after, a poor soldier, passing by the sea-beach, which was at a little distance from the woods which Timon frequented, found a tomb on the verge of the sea, with an inscription upon it, purporting that it was the grave of Timon the man-hater, who 'While he lived, did hate all living men, and dying wished a plague might consume all caitiffs left!'

Whether he finished his life by violence, or whether mere distaste of life and the loathing he had for mankind brought Timon to his conclusion, was not clear, yet all men admired the fitness of his epitaph, and the consistency of his end: dying, as he had lived, a hater of mankind; and some there were who fancied a conceit in the very choice which he had made of the sea-beach for his place of burial, where the vast sea might weep for ever upon his grave, as in contempt of the transient and shallow tears of hypocritical and deceitful mankind.

6

MACBETH

INTRODUCTION

Macbeth is a tale of a man of the highest promise and potential brought down by the dark forces that encircle and inhabit the human soul.

The mysterious power of this work has overspilled its fictional perimeter: the play was allegedly cursed by a coven of witches in revenge for Shakespeare including in it real spells, and theatrical lore has it that speaking the name 'Macbeth' inside a theatre will cause disaster (for which reason the play is often instead referred to as 'the Scottish play').

The tale opens with Macbeth and his companion, Banquo, returning victorious from wars against a rebel army. On a barren heath they encounter three 'weird sisters' (witches) who address Macbeth first by the title of Thane of Glamis (which he was), then Thane of Cawdor, and then as 'king that shalt be hereafter', before prophesizing that Banquo's sons shall be kings of Scotland. The weird sisters vanish into thin air, but shortly thereafter Macbeth is made Thane of Cawdor in recognition for his services, as had been predicted. Returning to his castle, Macbeth discusses the matter with his wife, and when King Duncan comes to spend the night the pair hatch a plan to murder the King and blame his death on his two grooms. The plan is put into effect, Macbeth kills the King, and the King's sons, Malcolm and Donalbain, flee Scotland for England and Ireland respectively. But Macbeth, despite having obtained the kingship, is unable to rest secure in his newfound majesty. Haunted by the prospect that Banquo's sons will become kings, Macbeth arranges for the murder of Banquo and his son Fleance, but although Banquo is killed, Fleance escapes. Macbeth now descends further into tyranny. Malcolm, meanwhile, has raised an army, which he brings to Scotland against the usurper. Macbeth is defeated and killed, but not without making one valiant last stand against insurmountable odds.

Macbeth is a tale, above all, of ambition: what does it give us and where, ultimately, does it lead? Ambition rarely confers satisfaction: we are always attracted by what is difficult to obtain, and yet—once attained—the objects of our ambition so often seem to lose their lustre. The initial elevation of Macbeth from Thane of Glamis to Thane of Cawdor provides, at most, an infinitesimally brief moment of pleasure for Macbeth, for the instant he is informed of it his mind races forward to the next challenge. Ambition also rarely confers security: in order to satisfy one's ambition, the object of such must be attainable; but if the object is attainable, then it is likely to be attainable by others too. *Macbeth* displays this logic at its most intense, since its protagonist has demonstrated by his own ruthlessness and disloyalty towards King Duncan that he will always be vulnerable, as king, to men as ruthless as himself. Better than any other figure in literary history, Macbeth embodies and displays what ambition brings: a base state of restlessness, punctuated by momentary triumph, followed by gnawing dissatisfaction and deep-seated insecurity.

Macbeth is also a tale about man's role in the universe. In Christian theology, there has always been a question as to how to reconcile an all-powerful and all-knowing creator with human free will and personal responsibility. The same duality appears in the overlapping supernatural and psychological realities that we see in *Macbeth*: Macbeth is haunted both in the supernatural sense and in the psychological sense, in that he encounters what appear to be supernatural beings with unnatural skills (supernatural reality) while on other occasions he sees things that no-one else sees, such as the dagger in the air or the ghost of Banquo (psychological reality). This begs the question: is Macbeth's end foreordained by supernatural forces or is it a result of personal characteristics and drives for which he alone is ultimately responsible? Of course, if each of the predictions of the weird sisters comes to fruition—as each does—then we might conclude that free will and personal responsibility are overborne by supernatural or providential dispensation. However, let us not forget that if the weird sisters' prophecy had indeed been determinative, then there would have been no need for further action on Macbeth's part—but he decided, anyway, to take matters into his own hands. In fact, in *Macbeth*, it is man's freely choosing a course of action that makes the prophecy come true.

Like all great Shakespearean tragedies, we finish Macbeth with a sense not merely of loss and devastation, but also of awe. Macbeth the man is a totally flawed individual: he is ruthless, cruel, opportunistic, disloyal, and treacherous. At the same time, by the close of his story, he comes across as a colossal figure. Whereas so many of us live from beginning to end on the surface of life, never losing greatly because never daring greatly, Macbeth has staked and lost everything. Many in such circumstances are crushed and defeated. Macbeth in adversity is at his best. He becomes philosophical; no longer merely a warrior, he produces some of Shakespeare's greatest verse:

Life's but a walking shadow, a poor player
That struts and frets his hour upon the stage
And then is heard no more. It is a tale

Told by an idiot, full of sound and fury,
Signifying nothing.

Above all, by the very end of his life he is reconciled
to what has become of himself. If die he must, he will
die fighting. He has come home to himself and the
four words that begin his final speech tell us all we
need to know of him: *I will not yield.*

MACBETH

When Duncan the Meek reigned King of Scotland, there lived a great thane, or lord, called Macbeth. This Macbeth was a near kinsman to the King, and in great esteem at court for his valour and conduct in the wars; an example of which he had lately given, in defeating a rebel army assisted by the troops of Norway in terrible numbers.

The two Scottish generals, Macbeth and Banquo, returning victorious from this great battle, their way lay over a blasted heath, where they were stopped by the strange appearance of three figures like women, except that they had beards, and their withered skins and wild attire made them look not like any earthly creatures. Macbeth first addressed them, when they, seemingly offended, laid each one her choppy finger upon her skinny lips, in token of silence; and the first of them saluted Macbeth with the title of Thane of Glamis. The general was not a little startled to find himself known by such creatures; but how much more, when the second of them followed up that salute by giving him the title of Thane of Cawdor, to which honour he had no pretensions; and again the third bid him 'All hail! King that shalt be hereafter!' Such a prophetic greeting might well amaze him, who knew that while the King's sons lived he could not hope to succeed to the throne. Then turning to Banquo, they pronounced him, in a sort of riddling terms, to be lesser than Macbeth and greater! not so happy, but much happier! and prophesied that though he should never reign, yet his sons after him should be kings in Scotland. They then turned into air, and vanished: by which the generals knew them to be the weird sisters, or witches. While they stood pondering on the strangeness of this adventure, there arrived certain messengers from the King, who were empowered by him to confer upon Macbeth the dignity of Thane of Cawdor. An event so miraculously corresponding with the prediction of the witches astonished Macbeth, and he stood wrapped in amazement, unable to make reply to the messengers; and in that point of time swelling hopes arose in his mind that the prediction of the third witch might in like manner have its accomplishment, and that he should one day reign king in Scotland.

Turning to Banquo, he said: 'Do you not hope that your children shall be kings, when what the witches promised to me has so wonderfully come to pass?' 'That hope,' answered the general, 'might enkindle you to aim at the throne; but oftentimes these ministers of darkness tell us truths in little things to betray us into deeds of greatest consequence.'

But the wicked suggestions of the witches had sunk too deep into the mind of Macbeth to allow him to attend to the warnings of the good Banquo. From that time he bent all his thoughts on how to compass the throne of Scotland.

Macbeth had a wife, to whom he communicated the strange prediction of the weird sisters, and its partial accomplishment. She was a bad, ambitious woman, and so as her husband and herself could arrive at greatness she cared not much by what means. She spurred on the reluctant purpose of Macbeth, who felt compunction at the thoughts of blood, and did not cease to represent the murder of the King as a step absolutely necessary to the fulfilment of the flattering prophecy.

It happened at this time that the King, who out

of his royal condescension would oftentimes visit his principal nobility upon gracious terms, came to Macbeth's house, attended by his two sons, Malcolm and Donalbain, and a numerous train of thanes and attendants, the more to honour Macbeth for the triumphal success of his wars.

The castle of Macbeth was pleasantly situated, and the air about it was sweet and wholesome, which appeared by the nests which the martlet, or swallow, had built under all the jutting friezes and buttresses of the building, wherever it found a place of advantage: for where those birds most breed and haunt the air is observed to be delicate. The King entered well-pleased with the place, and not less so with the attentions and respect of his honoured hostess, Lady Macbeth, who had the art of covering treacherous purposes with smiles; and could look like the innocent flower, while she was indeed the serpent under it.

The King, being tired with his journey, went early to bed, and in his state-room two grooms of his chamber (as was the custom) slept beside him. He had been unusually pleased with his reception, and had made presents before he retired to his principal officers; and among the rest, had sent a rich diamond to Lady Macbeth, greeting her by the name of his most kind hostess.

Now was the middle of night, when over half the world nature seems dead, and wicked dreams abuse men's minds asleep, and none but the wolf and the murderer is abroad. This was the time when Lady Macbeth waked to plot the murder of the King.

She would not have undertaken a deed so abhorrent to her sex, but that she feared her husband's nature, that it was too full of the milk of human kindness to do a contrived murder. She knew him to be ambitious, but withal to be scrupulous, and not yet prepared for that height of crime which commonly in the end accompanies inordinate ambition. She had won him to consent to the murder, but she doubted his resolution; and she feared that the natural tenderness of his disposition (more humane than her own) would come between and defeat the purpose.

So with her own hands armed with a dagger she approached the King's bed; having taken care to ply the grooms of his chamber so with wine that they slept intoxicated, and careless of their charge. There lay Duncan, in a sound sleep after the fatigues of his journey, and as she viewed him earnestly, there was something in his face, as he slept, which resembled her own father; and she had not the courage to proceed.

She returned to confer with her husband. His resolution had begun to stagger. He considered that there were strong reasons against the deed. In the first place, he was not only a subject, but a near kinsman to the King; and he had been his host and entertainer that day, whose duty, by the laws of hospitality, it was to shut the door against his murderers, not bear the knife himself. Then he considered how just and merciful a king this Duncan had been, how clear of offence to his subjects, how loving to his nobility, and in particular to him; that such kings are the peculiar care of Heaven, and their subjects doubly bound to revenge their deaths. Besides, by the favours of the King, Macbeth stood high in the opinion of all sorts of men, and how would those honours be stained by the reputation of so foul a murder!

In these conflicts of the mind Lady Macbeth found her husband inclining to the better part, and resolving to proceed no further. But she, being a woman not easily shaken from her evil purpose, began to pour in at his ears words which infused a portion of her own spirit into his mind, assigning reason upon reason why he should not shrink from what he had undertaken; how easy the deed was; how soon it would be over; and how the action of one short night would give to all their nights and days to come sovereign sway and royalty!

Then she threw contempt on his change of purpose, and accused him of fickleness and cowardice; and declared that she had given suck, and knew how tender it was to love the babe that milked her; but she would, while it was smiling in her face, have plucked it from her breast, and dashed its brains out, if she had so sworn to do it, as he had sworn to perform that murder. Then she added how practicable it was to lay the guilt of the deed upon the drunken sleepy grooms. And with the valour of her tongue she so chastised his sluggish resolutions that he once more summoned up courage to the bloody business.

So, taking the dagger in his hand, he softly stole in the dark to the room where Duncan lay; and as he went, he thought he saw another dagger in the air, with the handle towards him, and on the blade and at the point of it drops of blood; but when he tried to grasp at it, it was nothing but air, a mere phantasm proceeding from his own hot and oppressed brain and the business he had in hand.

Getting rid of this fear, he entered the King's room, whom he dispatched with one stroke of his dagger. Just as he had done the murder, one of the grooms, who slept in the chamber, laughed in his sleep, and the other cried, 'Murder,' which woke them both; but they said a short prayer; one of them said, 'God bless us!' and the other answered, 'Amen'; and addressed themselves to sleep again. Macbeth, who stood listening to them, tried to say 'Amen' when the fellow said 'God bless us!' but, though he had most need of a blessing, the word stuck in his throat, and he could not pronounce it.

Again he thought he heard a voice which cried, 'Sleep no more: Macbeth doth murder sleep, the innocent sleep, that nourishes life.' Still it cried, 'Sleep no more,' to all the house. 'Glamis hath murdered sleep, and therefore Cawdor shall sleep no more. Macbeth shall sleep no more.'

With such horrible imaginations Macbeth returned to his listening wife, who began to think he had failed of his purpose, and that the deed was somehow frustrated. He came in so distracted a state that she reproached him with his want of firmness, and sent him to wash his hands of the blood which stained them, while she took his dagger, with purpose to stain the cheeks of the grooms with blood, to make it seem their guilt.

Morning came, and with it the discovery of the murder, which could not be concealed; and though Macbeth and his lady made great show of grief, and the proofs against the grooms (the dagger being produced against them and their faces smeared with blood) were sufficiently strong, yet the entire suspicion fell upon Macbeth, whose inducements to such a deed were so much more forcible than such poor silly grooms could be supposed to have; and Duncan's two sons fled. Malcolm, the eldest, sought for refuge in the English court; and the youngest, Donalbain, made his escape to Ireland.

The King's sons, who should have succeeded him, having thus vacated the throne, Macbeth as next heir was crowned king, and thus the prediction of the weird sisters was literally accomplished.

Though placed so high, Macbeth and his queen could not forget the prophecy of the weird sisters that, though Macbeth should be king, yet not his children, but the children of Banquo, should be kings after him. The thought of this, and that they had defiled their hands with blood, and done so great crimes, only to place the posterity of Banquo upon the throne, so rankled within them that they determined to put to death both Banquo and his son, to make void the predictions of the weird sisters, which in their own case had been so remarkably brought to pass.

For this purpose they made a great supper, to which they invited all the chief thanes; and, among the rest, with marks of particular respect, Banquo and his son Fleance were invited. The way by which Banquo was to pass to the palace at night was beset by murderers appointed by Macbeth, who stabbed Banquo; but in the scuffle Fleance escaped. From that Fleance descended a race of monarchs who afterwards filled the Scottish throne, ending with James the Sixth of Scotland and the First of England, under whom the two crowns of England and Scotland were united.

At supper, the queen, whose manners were in the highest degree affable and royal, played the hostess with a gracefulness and attention which conciliated every one present, and Macbeth discoursed freely with his thanes and nobles, saying that all that was honourable in the country was under his roof, if he had but his good friend Banquo present, whom yet he hoped he should rather have to chide for neglect than to lament for any mischance. Just at these words the ghost of Banquo, whom he had caused to be murdered, entered the room and placed himself on the chair which Macbeth was about to occupy.

Though Macbeth was a bold man, and one that could have faced the devil without trembling, at this horrible sight his cheeks turned white with fear, and he stood quite unmanned with his eyes fixed upon the ghost.

His queen and all the nobles, who saw nothing but perceived him gazing (as they thought) upon an empty chair, took it for a fit of distraction; and she reproached him, whispering that it was but the same fancy which had made him see the dagger in the air when he was about to kill Duncan. But Macbeth continued to see the ghost, and gave no heed to all they could say, while he addressed it with distracted words, yet so significant, that his queen, fearing the dreadful secret would be disclosed, in great haste dismissed the guests, excusing the infirmity of Macbeth as a disorder he was often troubled with.

To such dreadful fancies Macbeth was subject. His queen and he had their sleeps afflicted with terrible dreams, and the blood of Banquo troubled them not more than the escape of Fleance, whom now they looked upon as father to a line of kings who should keep their posterity out of the throne. With these miserable thoughts they found no peace, and Macbeth determined once more to seek out the weird sisters, and know from them the worst. He sought them in a cave upon the heath, where they, who knew by foresight of his coming, were engaged in preparing their dreadful charms, by which they conjured up infernal spirits to reveal to them futurity. Their horrid ingredients were toads, bats, and serpents, the eye of a newt and the tongue of a dog, the leg of a lizard and the wing of the night-owl, the scale of a dragon, the tooth of a wolf, the maw of the ravenous salt-sea shark, the mummy of a witch, the root of the poisonous hemlock (this to have effect must be digged in the dark), the gall of a goat and the liver of a Jew, with slips of the yew tree that roots itself in graves, and the finger of a dead child: all these were set on to boil in a great kettle, or cauldron, which, as fast as it grew too hot, was cooled with a baboon's blood; to these they poured in the blood of a sow that had eaten her young, and they threw into the flame the grease that had sweaten from a murderer's gibbet. By these charms they bound the infernal spirits to answer their questions.

It was demanded of Macbeth whether he would have his doubts resolved by them, or by their masters, the spirits. He, nothing daunted by the dreadful ceremonies which he saw, boldly answered: 'Where are they? Let me see them.' And they called the spirits, which were three. And the first arose in the likeness of an armed head, and he called Macbeth by name, and bid him beware of the Thane of Fife; for which caution Macbeth thanked him: for Macbeth had entertained a jealousy of Macduff, the Thane of Fife.

And the second spirit arose in the likeness of a

bloody child, and he called Macbeth by name, and bid him have no fear, but laugh to scorn the power of man, for none of woman born should have power to hurt him; and he advised him to be bloody, bold, and resolute. 'Then live, Macduff!' cried the King. 'What need I fear of thee? But yet I will make assurance doubly sure. Thou shalt not live; that I may tell pale-hearted fear it lies, and sleep in spite of thunder.'

That spirit being dismissed, a third arose in the form of a child crowned, with a tree in his hand. He called Macbeth by name, and comforted him against conspiracies, saying that he should never be vanquished until the wood of Birnam to Dunsinane Hill should come against him. 'Sweet bodements! Good!' cried Macbeth: 'Who can unfix the forest, and move it from its earth-bound roots? I see I shall live the usual period of man's life, and not be cut off by a violent death. But my heart throbs to know one thing. Tell me, if your art can tell so much, if Banquo's issue shall ever reign in this kingdom?' Here the cauldron sunk into the ground, and a noise of music was heard, and eight shadows, like kings, passed by Macbeth, and Banquo last, who bore a glass which showed the figures of many more, and Banquo all bloody smiled upon Macbeth, and pointed to them; by which Macbeth knew that these were the posterity of Banquo, who should reign after him in Scotland; and the witches, with a sound of soft music, and with dancing, making a show of duty and welcome to

Macbeth, vanished. And from this time the thoughts of Macbeth were all bloody and dreadful.

The first thing he heard when he got out of the witches' cave was that Macduff, Thane of Fife, had fled to England to join the army which was forming against him under Malcolm, the eldest son of the late king, with intent to displace Macbeth, and set Malcolm, the rightful heir, upon the throne. Macbeth, stung with rage, set upon the castle of Macduff, and put his wife and children, whom the Thane had left behind, to the sword, and extended the slaughter to all who claimed the least relationship to Macduff.

These and suchlike deeds alienated the minds of all his chief nobility from him. Such as could, fled to join with Malcolm and Macduff, who were now approaching with a powerful army, which they had raised in England; and the rest secretly wished success to their arms, though for fear of Macbeth they could take no active part. His recruits went on slowly. Everybody hated the tyrant; nobody loved or honoured him; but all suspected him, and he began to envy the condition of Duncan, whom he had murdered, who slept soundly in his grave, against whom treason had done its worst: neither steel nor poison, domestic malice nor foreign levies, could hurt him any longer.

While these things were acting, the queen, who had been the sole partner in his wickedness, in whose bosom he could sometimes seek a momentary repose from those terrible dreams which afflicted them both nightly, died, it is supposed by her own hands, unable to bear the remorse of guilt, and public hate; by which event he was left alone, without a soul to love or care for him, or a friend to whom he could confide his wicked purposes.

He grew careless of life, and wished for death; but the near approach of Malcolm's army roused in him what remained of his ancient courage, and he determined to die (as he expressed it) 'with armour on his back.' Besides this, the hollow promises of the witches had filled him with a false confidence, and he remembered the sayings of the spirits, that none of woman born was to hurt him, and that he was never to be vanquished till Birnam wood should come to Dunsinane, which he thought could never be. So he shut himself up in his castle, whose impregnable strength was such as defied a siege: here he sullenly awaited the approach of Malcolm. When, upon a day, there came a messenger to him, pale and shaking with fear, almost unable to report that which he had seen: for he averred that as he stood upon his watch on the hill, he looked towards Birnam, and to his thinking the wood began to move! 'Liar and slave!' cried Macbeth. 'If thou speakest false thou shalt hang alive upon the next tree, till famine end thee. If thy tale be true, I care not if thou dost as much by me.' For Macbeth now began to faint in resolution, and to doubt the equivocal speeches of the spirits. He was not to fear till Birnam wood should come to Dunsinane; and now a wood did move! 'However,' said he, 'if this which he avouches be true, let us arm and out. There is no flying hence, nor staying here. I begin to be weary of the sun, and wish my life at an end.' With these desperate speeches he sallied forth upon the besiegers, who had now come up to the castle.

The strange appearance, which had given the messenger an idea of a wood moving, is easily solved. When the besieging army marched through the wood of Birnam, Malcolm, like a skilful general, instructed his soldiers to hew down every one a bough and bear it before him, by way of concealing the true numbers of his host. This marching of the soldiers with boughs had at a distance the appearance which had frightened the messenger. Thus were the words of the spirit brought to pass, in a sense different from that in which Macbeth had understood them, and one great hold of his confidence was gone.

And now a severe skirmishing took place, in which Macbeth, though feebly supported by those who called themselves his friends, but in reality hated the tyrant and inclined to the party of Malcolm and Macduff, yet fought with the extreme of rage and valour, cutting to pieces all who were opposed to him, till he came to where Macduff was fighting. Seeing Macduff, and remembering the caution of the spirit, who had counselled him to avoid Macduff above all men, he would have turned, but Macduff, who had been seeking him through the whole fight, opposed his turning, and a fierce contest ensued; Macduff giving him many foul reproaches for the murder of his wife and children. Macbeth, whose soul was charged enough with blood of that family already, would still have declined the combat; but Macduff still urged him to it, calling him tyrant, murderer, hell-hound, and villain.

Then Macbeth remembered the words of the spirit, how none of woman born should hurt him; and smiling confidently he said to Macduff, 'Thou losest thy labour, Macduff. As easily thou mayest impress the air with thy sword, as make me vulnerable. I bear a charmed life, which must not yield to one of woman born.'

'Despair thy charm,' said Macduff, 'and let that lying spirit, whom thou hast served, tell thee, that Macduff was never born of woman, never as the ordinary manner of men is to be born, but was untimely taken from his mother.'

'Accursed be the tongue which tells me so,' said the trembling Macbeth, who felt his last hold of confidence give way, 'and let never man in future believe the lying equivocations of witches and juggling spirits, who deceive us in words which have double senses, and while they keep their promise literally, disappoint our hopes with a different meaning. I will not fight with thee.'

'Then live!' said the scornful Macduff. 'We will have a show of thee, as men show monsters, and a painted board, on which shall be written: *Here men may see the tyrant!'*

'Never,' said Macbeth, whose courage returned with despair. 'I will not live to kiss the ground before young Malcolm's feet, and to be baited with the curses of the rabble. Though Birnam wood be come to Dunsinane, and thou opposed to me, who wast never born of woman, yet will I try the last.' With these frantic words he threw himself upon Macduff, who, after a severe struggle, in the end overcame him, and, cutting off his head, made a present of it to the young and lawful king, Malcolm; who took upon him the government which, by the machinations of the usurper, he had so long been deprived of, and ascended the throne of Duncan the Meek, amid the acclamations of the nobles and the people.

Resources

Shakespeare Editions
For the complete works, the Oxford, Norton, and Riverside editions can all be recommended. For individual plays, as a general rule the Arden editions are excellent.

Shakespeare on Screen
There are cinematic versions of many of Shakespeare's plays, some of them excellent. The BBC have filmed all the plays for television as 'The Shakespeare Collection'.

Further Information and Resources
Further information on recommended texts, cinematic versions, and suggested reading can be found at www.andrewlynn.com.

Made in the
USA
Middletown, DE